Write of Passage

A Southerner's View of Then and Now

By John Moore

John Moore grew up in LA (Lower Arkansas) and now lives in East Texas, where he writes a weekly blog and newspaper column, and owns a voiceover recording studio. He spent over two decades in the radio business as an announcer and currently works in public relations and marketing. He and his wife enjoy quiet time on their acreage at the end of a dead-end road in the middle of nowhere.

Write of Passage

A Southerner's View of Then and Now

By John Moore

Thanks

My sincere appreciation to Elise for editing this manuscript. Thanks to my buddy, Emmitte, who helped me put the project together and listened to me sing off key during our guitar jam sessions.

The stories in this book are from memory. Any errors are solely mine.

Dedication

For Terry

Table of Contents

INTRODUCTION

I was born in the right place at the right time. I'm a Southerner and a Baby Boomer.

My upbringing included the work ethic and resourcefulness of grandparents who got our great country through the Depression and World War II, and parents who were able to provide me opportunities they hadn't had.

I went to school in the 1960s and '70s. It was an amazing time. We had the best bands. I got to see many of them live and hear their records for the first time on the radio.

Everyone who also grew up when I did knows how lucky we were. We enjoyed one of the best eras in American history.

Those who shared this time period have a special bond. I hope that this book helps the reader remember how great it truly was.

CHAPTER ONE – FAMILY MATTERS

Where I Come From

I grew up in the South. My family stock is one of honest laborers who made their livings through sweat and necessity. My mother's side chopped cotton on land that wasn't theirs. My father's family was comprised of blacksmiths and other similar trades.

Both sides were also homesteaders. In addition to long days of exhausting physical labor, family members from the youngest to the oldest would draw water from a well, split wood for the stove, help with the garden, and tend to the hogs and chickens that provided meat.

Feeding a family and getting by required the use of your back more than your brain.

My family was filled with very smart people, but labor was the work that was available. My father and mother would later push education for this reason.

Arkansas had two main industries at that time: poultry and pines.

Chicken houses dotted the landscape of my home state. To make their living, many a family set up large-scale chicken houses and sold their birds to processing plants.

Other men worked in logging. An incredibly dangerous profession, cutting and hauling trees could get you killed, and some were. The trees went to local sawmills to be turned into lumber. That was the case until the 1960s, when Nekoosa Paper Company built one of the finest paper mills in the world in my hometown. Then, the pines were also hauled to Nekoosa to make pulp for paper.

"The mill," as it was and still is called, with its low-hanging, acrid, smokestack output, filled Ashdown, Arkansas, with a ubiquitous stench and lots of jobs. Many men and women suddenly had an option to leave the fields and forests to make more money than they could have ever imagined.

The jobs at the mill required no college degree and came with great benefits. But, most people I knew who worked or still work there hold somewhere between a mild and great disdain for it. Whether it was the management or the shift work, I don't know. I just knew that the mill wasn't for me.

My future wasn't at the mill, or anywhere else in The Natural State. But, my memories of growing up and the lessons I learned in Little River County, Arkansas, are ones that shaped me into who I am today. A proud Southerner.

Gardens and Grandma

As a kid, I hated the vegetable garden. If you stood on our back porch, it was to your left. It took up the entire corner of our large yard.

To me, gardens were work and nothing more. From planting, to weeding, to harvesting, to canning, it was a waste of valuable playtime. It also took away the area of the yard that the neighborhood kids and I liked using for a baseball diamond.

I would watch television and see advertisements for Birds Eye Frozen Vegetables, Green Giant corn, beans and peas, and wonder why I had to help with something that the Jolly Green Giant was already doing. Besides, he was a giant, so he should be able to knock out our gardening needs in nothing flat. All we had to do was go to the Piggly Wiggly and buy what he offered.

Walking through the rows during each hot, Arkansas summer, the tomato and okra plants would make my skin itch. The mosquitoes from the nearby rice paddies would swarm, and I would try and swat them without spilling the vegetables that I had been instructed to pick and was precariously balancing in my hands and on my arms.

My grandmother would come to our house, and I was forced to sit and help shell peas. We would sit in a circle and my grandmother would put a round, porcelain wash pan on her lap.

She'd fill it with a stack of purple hulls and then one by one, pop the end from the pea pod and then rapidly run her thumb through it, putting the peas into a bowl on her left and then the empty pea pod into a Piggly Wiggly sack on the floor on her right. She did this in one seamless motion, over and over until she was done.

During the shelling, which could take hours, she would tell stories of her memories of doing the same thing with her grandparents and other long-since-passed ancestors of mine. She would tell me how much I would have liked one or the other. And how much they would have liked me.

I asked once why we needed so many vegetables.

"Oh, we don't," she said. "We will share the extra with those who can use them."

"What?" I thought. "Why are we doing all of this extra work for food we aren't even going to eat?"

I would patiently wait until we were finished and then ask if I could go outside and play.

I hated that garden.

When I grew up and married, I took Mr. Birds Eye and the Jolly Green Giant up on their generous offers. Buying vegetables was easy and convenient.

My children never had to endure a garden. I saw to that.

A year or so after the kids had left the nest, my wife asked me to clear out a square area behind our house that the previous owners had used to plant shrubs, flowers, or who knows what. It was bordered with old railroad cross ties, stacked three high.

If you stood on our back porch, it was to your left. It took up the entire corner of our large yard.

I cleared it of the weeds and rocks. I say rocks, but most of them were more like boulders.

When it was cleared, I looked at it and thought about what we could do with it. Since potatoes are my favorite food, I thought about how great it would be to be able to go outside and dig up some whenever I wanted to.

But, I couldn't remember how to grow them. So, I called my grandmother.

Using her instructions, we wound up with an amazing crop. My wife and I were quite pleased.

Several years passed. So did my grandmother.

When we moved to the country, our garden grew. My wife planted more and more things. Tomatoes, peppers, cantaloupe, and others edibles were added.

When our grandson visited each summer, he was engaged to help with the picking and harvesting. As he assisted, I would tell him of his ancestors; those in our family that I used to help with the garden.

I told him about how much he would have liked one or the other. And how much they would have liked him.

Moore's Blacksmith Shop

My grandfather's shop seemed cavernous. Every room was filled with tools that a man with a strong back could use to make a living and feed his family.

My grandfather was a blacksmith. His name was Parmer.

He was a product of the Great Depression. Born in 1918, he arrived at adulthood in the midst of the worst economic period in American history. But, like many men and women of that era, he was raised in a family that survived not on money (they had very little), but on knowledge and hard work.

No doubt, the Depression affected him, but families were more self-reliant then. What you ate, you raised or grew. Your land provided your sustenance, and your family and friends taught you a trade.

Parmer's father was also a blacksmith. In his father's shop, my grandfather learned blacksmithing. He apprenticed under his father until he was good enough to move away and start his own business.

For the next 40 years, the hammer and anvil were his living.

My earliest memories of his shop are of him holding a cup of percolator coffee, the 7 Up machine sitting near the big front doors, the Frostie Root Beer clock that hung above it, and the radio next to the clock. As I would follow him from room to room, Patsy Cline, Faron Young, Loretta Lynn and other country music stars would sing to us.

I watched him work. It seemed there wasn't anything he couldn't do.

His customers would arrive with something broken, and they would leave with it fixed. It made me proud.

He could repair plows, replace hoe, axe or rake handles, and he could weld.

Before modern arc welders, which require electricity, there was the blacksmith. I was fortunate to witness a period where the old and the new converged. My grandfather did use an arc welder; but more often than not, he would fire up his coal forge and weld the old-fashioned way.

Heating up two pieces of metal and hammering them together on an anvil is the original way to weld.

He welcomed me to learn how he did it. I would watch as the fire in the forge turned the coal into glowing mounds. He would take a piece of stock metal, sometimes round, sometimes square, stick it in the forge and heat it until it was just the right color. He'd then move the metal he was working to

16

the anvil where he'd firmly hold it with his left hand and come down hard on it with the hammer in his right.

His left hand would turn the metal as he worked, allowing the hammer to shape it into what he wanted. When the metal would cool, he'd place it back in the forge and heat it up again, and then move back to the anvil. He continued until he had what he wanted.

Near the forge was a grinder. Under the grinder was a small washtub that he kept full of water. When he was done making what he wanted, he would dip the still-hot piece of metal in that tub. I can still hear the sound it made when that hot metal made contact with the cold water.

My grandfather believed in self-reliance. Instead of buying a replacement part, he made his own. Never buy anything that you could make yourself.

Even the sign on his building, which read, "Moore's Blacksmith Shop," was made of a piece of recycled metal.

He built his own forge. The bottom was a repurposed porcelain oil company sign, and the outer trim was a metal wagon wheel ring.

From the time of my first memories of him until I was 15, my grandfather taught me how to be my own man. He left us suddenly, way too young, at age 60.

Unable to bear the sight of his shop, my grandmother sold off its contents and had the building torn down. After the shop was gone, the remaining concrete slab finally revealed to me how small his shop actually was. Staring at the slab when I was older, I realized that it wasn't the physical footprint he had left that mattered. It was his God-given ability that had made the difference in so many lives.

My father was given one of the anvils and the shop sign, which a few years ago, he gave to me. Receiving these treasured items, I set them up in my shop and signed up for a blacksmithing class. I began to wonder what had happened to the forge.

My mother remembered who had bought it. Ironically, it was the doctor who had delivered me. But the doctor had passed away not long after my grandfather. I began my search to reunite the anvil and the forge. Amazingly, I was able to track down the doctor's grandson in Houston. I explained to him who I was and that I wanted to buy it back. He remembered where the forge was. It still sat in the same barn in Ashdown, Arkansas, where his grandfather had placed it the day he bought it. He agreed to sell it to me. I traveled to the barn and retrieved it.

It almost seemed as if the forge had been placed there to wait for me to one day find it and bring it home.

On weekends now, I like to head down to my shop early in the morning with a cup of percolator coffee. I open the big front doors and turn on the radio. Patsy Cline, Faron Young and Loretta Lynn sing to me.

Thanks to what my grandfather taught me, some days I use his old anvil to make or repair a part I need instead of buying one.

The sign resting above the anvil is faded, but it still clearly reads, "Moore's Blacksmith Shop."

Seeing Double

My mom is an identical twin. My mom's mom was also an identical twin.

There were at least two other sets of twins in my family when I was growing up: one identical, the other fraternal. So, growing up around people who looked exactly like each other seemed perfectly normal to me.

However, the rest of the world seems mesmerized by this fairly common gift from nature.

Wikipedia indicates that out of every 1,000 births in America, about 33 are twins.

The most common are fraternal (children who are not identical), with a boy/girl combination happening more than two boys or two girls.

For obvious reasons, identical twins get the most attention, as is the case with my mom and my aunt.

People have asked me some pretty silly questions about my mother and her twin sister. My personal favorite is, "How can you tell them apart?"

As if I only vaguely know my own mother.

In talking with other folks who have twins in their family, I'm told that they've also received some pretty goofy questions. The best one being, "Are they identical?" when referring to boy/girl twins.

When I was about 10, my mom worked for a savings and loan downtown. In the same building, but just around the corner, her twin sister worked for the revenue office. In Arkansas, the revenue office is where you go to get your driver's license.

More than once, my mom and her sister would tell the story of someone who came into the savings and loan to withdraw money, and then went around the corner to renew their driver's license.

"Hey, weren't you just in the bank next door giving me my money?" they'd ask my aunt.

Though both retired now, the two never seem to tire of telling that story.

20

The names that parents give their twins almost always seem to be as similar as their offspring. My mom and aunt are Mary Lou and Sarah Sue. Their mom and her twin were Leona and Viola.

I have identical twin cousins named, Arlene and Darlene.

Can you tell we're from the South?

Everything you've ever heard about twins being close is true. I've witnessed it my entire life. My mom and her sister think alike. They are completely in tune with each other. If something is wrong with one of them, innately, the other one seems to sense it.

Call it what you will, but it's real. I'll vouch for it.

There are many celebrities who have twins, but most folks don't know about them. Actors Marilu Henner, Billy Dee Williams, Ashton Kutcher, Kiefer Sutherland, and Linda Hamilton have twin siblings.

And twins certainly aren't a new thing. Isaac and Rebekah from the Bible had Jacob and Esau.

But my favorite celebrity identical twins are our grandsons. And yes, I can tell them apart.

The Canning Jar Quest

In the early 1970s, my mother began collecting a series of antique canning jars. I can't remember why this happened, but my best guess is that she came across one that was unique, she liked it, and she bought it.

This purchase would start a chain reaction and a multi-year search for my family.

Specifically, she sought green Atlas jars with glass lids. These were also known as "lightning jars." Allegedly, the name came from how much faster they were to open than the previous design for canning jars.

Unlike the canning jars with a screw-on metal lid, the lightning jars utilized a rubber ring and a metal clamp mechanism to hold the lid and seal in place.

From what little information I could find, the green Atlas lightning jars seemed to have been commonly made through the early 1900s, but they were never manufactured in the same quantities as the clear jars.

My information may not be accurate on this, but one thing is certain: By the early 1970s, finding green canning jars was difficult.

My mom first found a green, half-gallon lightning jar. That was the jar that began the quest for the rest.

Then she found the green quart and pint sizes. The old-timers told her that a green, half-pint jar had also been made. But, no one had seen one in years or knew where to find one.

The Internet was still more than two decades in the future, so auctions, letters to manufacturers, word of mouth, and searching garage, estate and junk sales were the ways we looked for one. Our monthly trip from Arkansas to Canton Trade Days was also a time that we would look.

Back then, Canton was nothing like it is today. Most booths featured true antiques and collectibles. You could barter or pay cash. Today, most things at Canton are arts, crafts, or new items and the prices are retail. I miss the old Canton.

At Trade Days, we scoured each booth for that jar.

In my youth, my family called me "Johnny." So, when we would arrive at Canton, my dad would remind each of us of our search for what was, at the time, the holy grail: a green, half-pint Atlas canning jar.

"Johnny, if you see one, come get your mother or me immediately," he would say.

"Yes, sir," I would respond.

The longer and harder we searched, the less likely it seemed that we would find one.

Maybe those who claimed to have seen a half-pint, Atlas lightning jar had just imagined it? Maybe what they remembered was a pint size. No, they were sure of it. They made a green, half-pint jar. They existed.

At least two years passed. Saturday night auctions in Broken Bow, Oklahoma, brought no luck. Neither did searching junk shops in Texarkana, Hot Springs, or the Dallas area.

It seemed that the possibility of us finding this jar was about as likely as us finding the actual Holy Grail.

One hot, summer day, we had walked Canton from front to back and decided to eat a hamburger before we left to head back home to the Natural State.

There was one particular hamburger stand we all enjoyed near what we called "the hill," which was located near the front gate.

We were disposing of our wrappers and cups when my dad said, "Hold on a minute. Everyone stay here. I'll be right back." He then disappeared around the corner of a building.

Standing in the hot sun, I was hoping that whatever he was doing, he would be quick about it.

He reappeared and called us all to follow him. We walked around the building and up to a booth. It was a small booth, with mostly junk on the tables. I couldn't figure out what had caught his eye.

24

And then I saw it. Near the side and back of a table, there it was. A green, half-pint Atlas jar.

It did exist.

My father and mother discussed the price. I don't remember how much the dealer wanted for it, but it must have been a lot for the time because there was some hesitation.

But, after that long of a search, I had little doubt that we would leave without it.

My dad negotiated a price, and the jar went home with us. It still resides at my parents' home, alongside the other three Atlas jars, and her collection of lady head vases and Aladdin lamps.

On the ride home from Canton, there was a sense of satisfaction and completion. But for me, it was bittersweet. A family-shared quest was now over.

Today, if you have the money and an Internet connection, you can find just about anything you want and have someone deliver it to your front door the next day.

But that convenience will never be as rewarding as working together as a family to find something that brings an amazing level of joy to your mom.

Grannies and Pappaws

When I was a kid, I didn't appreciate my grandparents as much as I should have. It's a mistake I think most of us make.

Grandparents and grandchildren share a bond. Innately, grandchildren know that there's a special love between them and their parents' parents.

Your mom and dad had your back, but your grandparents had your mom and dad's back. You always knew that.

I can remember my grandmother helping me on a school project for history class. I have fond memories of my other grandmother making the most amazing oatmeal. It was my grandfather who taught me how to use a riding lawnmower. And my other grandfather was a blacksmith who showed me the way around a shop.

My mom's parents showed God's love by hosting a number of foster children. My father's parents were also godly people who helped others in their time of need. Mostly, I remember my grandparents always having time for me.

I believe that there is no purer love than the love between grandparents and grandchildren.

Now that my wife and I have our own grandkids, I understand and can completely appreciate how my grandparents felt about me and all of my cousins all those years ago.

I was born the oldest grandchild on both sides of the family, so I not only witnessed their love for me, but I watched it grow with each of their other grandchildren. And there were lots of them. I have over 30 cousins.

Whenever I talk with one of my cousins these days, and unfortunately that isn't as often as it should be, inevitably the topic of one of our grandparents comes up. "Remember how good granny's biscuits were?" "Remember the percolator being plugged in all day and as they shared coffee, hearing our grandfather tell our grandmother how pretty she was?"

I was 15 when I lost my first grandparent. I was almost 50 when I lost my last one. Over the years, I called the remaining three frequently, and visited them whenever I went back home.

I miss being able to pick up the phone and ask them how to grow potatoes, or a fill in an answer with a question about ancestry.

In the 1980s, I set up my VHS camcorder and interviewed my three surviving grandparents. I asked them all of the questions you would ask of someone you were meeting for the first time. "What is your full name?" "Where were you born?" "Who are your brothers and sisters?" "Tell me about your children." "What was your childhood like?"

When my mother's mom passed away at age 89, I pulled the tape out and made a video tribute to her, which we played at her memorial. The video allowed her to tell her own story in her own words. One of the questions I asked at the end of the video is, "What do you want your descendants, whom you'll never meet, to know?"

She said, "I want them to know the Lord."

It brought tears, but it also brought happiness and great memories.

My wife and I have six grandchildren. Our love for all of them is endless. My hope is that one day, when they are grandparents, they'll look back as fondly at our relationship as we do.

CHAPTER TWO – BACK IN MY DAY

Pickin' Up Pop Bottles

When Richard Nixon was president, my sister and I would collect pop bottles that people tossed out of their cars. Deep ditches were a pop bottle gold mine.

Back then, pop bottles were made of green glass and were returned, washed and reused. People brag about recycling aluminum cans and plastic bottles these days, but back then, aluminum cans were not common. Everything came in glass.

The bottles were worth 5 cents each, which was a princely sum for a kid. A nickel would buy you a Charms Sucker, a package of LifeSavers or five pieces of Bazooka Bubble Gum. Bazooka Joe was the gum's mascot and his adventure cartoons were included on the wrapper of each piece. You could read the two-panel comic in about the same amount of time it took the flavor to leave the gum.

We'd clean the dirty pop bottles before we cashed them in at the Shur Way, because Coca-Cola and the other manufacturers of "soda water," as my grandmother called it, wouldn't take dirty ones. On good days, we'd each come home with a quarter, plus candy.

The bonus of any trip to cash in pop bottles was to find money people had dropped in the parking lot.

Most of the time, you can hear a coin when it hits the pavement, so we rarely found anything larger than a penny. That was because back then people would bend over to pick up most coins. But, if their arms were full or they were in a hurry, they left the pennies.

For pop-bottle-collecting kids, whoever found pennies had the bragging rights for the day, even if they'd cashed in more pop bottles. Because free money trumped pop-bottle money.

All of this came back to me recently when I found a dime in the parking lot of a convenience store. I'm not sure whether the person heard it hit the pavement or not; but if they did, they didn't think it was worth picking up.

I thought, "A dime. Nowadays, people don't even pick up dimes?"

I looked in the store for some Bazooka Bubble Gum to buy with my free dime, but didn't find any. Checking the Internet, I discovered the company no longer makes it. However, I did find a company that still has some of the last batch for sale.

I'm going to order some. I plan on paying for part of it with my free dime.

The Corner Store

Before Walmart and its supercenters, there were corner stores. A typical corner store was locally owned, small, sparsely stocked with kitchen and other household essentials, sometimes selling gasoline, and was located in or near the middle of a neighborhood.

In my hometown, we had Puckett's Store and Withem's Store. Both were located on Highway 32, with the former on the edge of town and the latter closer to the center.

My family traded primarily with Mr. Withem. In hindsight, that choice had a lot to do with proximity. Withem's Store was within walking distance from my grandparents' house, and was near the clinic, drug store, and other locations my family frequented.

I recall Mr. Withem as a thin man who, like many of his age in that era, went out of his way to be kind to children.

With my sister and me in tow, my mother would frequently stop at his store on the way home from my grandparents' house, to pick up a pound of bologna and other items.

As we waited for Mr. Withem to cut the whole stick bologna into the thick slices my dad preferred, I would stare at the advertisements that were inside his store.

In that era, companies eagerly provided advertising items such as clocks, thermometers and neon signs that incorporated the name of the company and the name of the corner store. This provided free promotion for their products and free signage for the storeowner, so it was a win-win for everyone.

For example, a sign on the door might read, "Come on in, it's KOOL inside." This would advertise KOOL cigarettes while also promoting the fact that a store had air conditioning. A Grapette Soda thermometer might hang near the drink cooler. One or two round Coca-Cola signs might hang on the front of the building. Esso, Standard Oil signs, or Mobil Oil's flying Pegasus might adorn the gas pumps.

These items are now considered Americana memorabilia and are highly collected and can be quite valuable.

Withem's Store had a lot of these types of corporate advertising pieces, but what I remember especially well is the entire back wall of Mr. Withem's meat market. It was a mural of Elsie The Cow's family. Elsie was and still is the symbol for Borden's Milk. As he sliced our cold cuts, Mr. Withem's would ask me to name the members of Elsie's family.

Elsie was the mom, but can you name the dad and their children? Elmer was the dad (when he wasn't helping his wife sell milk, he had another job selling Elmer's Glue for the company's chemical division), and Beulah and Beauregard were their children. Later, according to some research I did on the web, Elmer and Elsie had twins named Larabee and Lobelia. The mural in Mr. Withem's store must have predated the twins. They weren't included.

After I had named off Elsie's family, Mr. Withem would hand my mom our pound of bologna, all neatly packaged and taped in white butcher paper. He'd ring up the meat, and usually a gallon of milk, a loaf of Holsom Bread and a bag of Fritos, thank us, and send us on our way.

After my family moved to another part of town, we began trading at Shur Way Grocery, which was a few blocks from our new home. Owned by the Pope family, Shur Way was bigger than a corner store, but not as big as a supermarket.

When I was older, I remember mom sending me on my bike to pick up the same pound of bologna and other items and being told to, "Put it on our ticket."

This was during a time when businesses could trust you to run a tab and pay them once a month. Shur Way had a long board with slots, and the slots had springs that held each family's ticket in place. No debit cards, no checks, not even cash was needed. Neighbors trusted and did business with each other.

I still try to trade with locally owned businesses. It reminds me of people who supported my family when I was growing up, and it just feels a whole lot better than the self-checkout at Walmart.

Harvest Gold and Avocado Green

I grew up in the land of harvest gold and avocado green. I can withstand anything.

As a kid of the '70s, I was surrounded by bold colors and shag carpet. Most kids probably didn't notice or care how garish our surroundings were, but I did.

What were we thinking?

As a child, I would look at photos from the previous decades and admire the choices people made when they decorated their homes and businesses. Specifically, I was drawn to the Art Deco period.

I still think the design era that gave us the Empire State Building and radios that were pieces of furniture is one of the most symmetrically beautiful our country has ever had.

Even the 1940s offered amazing eye candy. Automobile manufacturers in the U.S. were still pairing teams of innovative people who worked to make not only each brand of car, but also each brand's models, unique and recognizable.

You knew a Ford or a Chevrolet or Buick when you saw one. Now, most cars have as much flair as a stump.

The 1950s continued with what was a distinctive American look. A Formica dinette table could be found in most homes. The patterns on the surface of the table and chairs were fun. People still love them. The same inexpensive table and chairs today, in good condition, can sell in the thousands.

But, in my humble opinion, it was the 1960s when the design wheels began to come off.

Big hair, cat-eye glasses and fake wood paneling were the beginning of the end. Once those caught on, it was inevitable that I would one day wind up going to my ninth-grade prom in a leisure suit.

My grandfather was buried in a leisure suit. I still shudder at the thought.

Not everything from the era was a fashion risk. I liked bell-bottom jeans, the 1972 Oldsmobile Cutlass Supreme, and Farrah Fawcett.

All three were quite acceptable and an important part of my teen years. Especially Farrah Fawcett.

But green and gold applied to shag carpet should never have been allowed to happen. I firmly believe that there was a guy somewhere who made the first sample as a joke, and people took him seriously.

But you can't put toothpaste back in the tube, and shag carpet wound up being with us for far too long.

Of course, how we decorate our homes these days, the clothes we wear, our hairstyles and more, will be judged by future generations, just as I now judge the 1970s.

How will the things we all seem to like now rank with our descendants?

Who knows?

As my dad says, "There just ain't no accountin' for taste."

A Free Gift Inside

My sister and I would make a beeline for the cereal aisle at the Piggly Wiggly while my mom did the shopping.

Decisions, decisions. Did we want to roll the dice and pick the cereal that promised the possibility of getting the coolest toy, or did we want to go with cereal we liked since, either way, we'd have to eat the whole box?

They were called product premiums, and you don't see them much anymore.

The marketers of American products used to know how to get the allegiance of consumers: Buy it. Many products, from cereal to laundry detergent to oatmeal to gasoline to jelly to snacks, once came with something free. A gift or prize, if you will.

It was genius. Many of the items were not only decent, today the items can be quite collectible and valuable.

One of the coolest items I remember getting from my mom buying us cereal wasn't in the box, it was on the box. Post and other cereal manufacturers would put an actual, playable record on the back of the box. This made it easy to see which one you wanted.

After you ate the whole box of cereal (mom made that mandatory), you were then allowed to take a pair of scissors and cut the record out. After some finagling, you would get the record as flat as possible and then listen to it on your record player.

I always avoided the Bobby Sherman records and went with the cereal that included an Archie's record. I liked to try and keep it real back then.

I always assumed that records on cereal boxes was something new to my time, but that wasn't the case. I've seen an example of a Mickey Mouse Club 78 RPM record from a box of Wheaties from 1956.

Oxydol used to offer premiums too. There might be anything from a glass to a dish to a towel in their boxes of laundry detergent. I'm sure they could never do that today. Breakable items in products would never pass the government's nosy intrusions into whether we want to take our own risks. Too bad.

Breeze was another laundry soap I remember that had towels or wash rags (or possibly both) inside the box.

I remember my grandmother buying a specific brand of oatmeal because it included a cup in each box. I'm not sure whether the cup was made of glass or plastic, I just recall that when you opened her cupboard to get something to get a drink with, there were lots of them in there.

That's a lot of oatmeal.

Before the oil embargo and long gas lines of the early 1970s, Texaco, Shell, Esso (the precursor to Exxon), Sinclair, Gulf, Union 76, and others offered premiums for fill-ups.

Texaco had "Fire Chief" gasoline, so they would offer a fire chief hat. What better way to get the children in the family to scream from the back seat where Dad or Mom should fill up the Buick than by offering a free fire chief hat?

Shell had a game with presidential coins where, if you got the right coins, you would win prizes. If I remember correctly, the prizes were cash. But, I don't remember anyone we knew ever getting a Martin Van Buren and hitting it big.

Esso had a fuzzy tiger tail that you could hang from your gas cap to show that you had a "Tiger in your tank," which was their ad slogan.

Sinclair gas stations, in addition to having a huge green dinosaur on the property that could be seen from great distances, also gave away green toy dinosaurs with a fill-up.

Gulf stations would give away small plastic horseshoes. They represented the extra horsepower that their gas supposedly provided your car's engine, but the horseshoes were also functional. They could actually be used to play the game.

But, probably the credit for smartest gas station giveaway went to Union 76. Back when everyone's car had a radio antenna, they would give you an orange ball that had a big "76" on it to go on top of it. It was a brilliant advertising strategy. Antenna toppers and many car antennas are now gone for the most part.

One of the few premiums that's still around today, and my wife and I still buy them, is jelly that comes in a jar with a handle. Blackburn's puts everything from jelly to jam to preserves in reusable, glass jars that have a handle. When you open our cupboard, it's full of them.

Cracker Jack (not Cracker Jacks, as we all tend to say it) used to always come with a "Toy surprise inside." It made you remember their jingle. "Candy-coated popcorn, peanuts and a prize. That's what you get in Cracker Jack!"

But from what I can tell, at some point, they stopped putting a prize in each box of Cracker Jack, and the toys were replaced with pieces of paper with jokes on them or directions to a website. How lame is that?

I miss the days of advertising premiums.
Blackburn's is one of the few companies that still
offers one and obviously still sees the effectiveness
of them.

Consequently, we eat a lot of jelly.

Stuck on Green Stamps

My mom and her mother saved 7 1/2 books to get us
that swing set. Just three years before in 1966, my
parents had saved to buy their first house. Money
was tight, so, if my sister and I were going to have
that new addition to the backyard, Green Stamps
would be the key.

For families in America in the 1960s and '70s,
Green Stamps were part of life.

S&H Green Stamps are no longer available, but at
their zenith, moms, children, and grandmothers
shopped at stores that offered Green Stamps as a
way to make ends meet and have something to look
forward to. If you saved enough Green Stamp books,
you could buy just about anything you wanted with
them.

According to a 2013 article by Greg Hatala at
nj.com, the Sperry and Hutchinson Company was
founded in 1896 by Thomas Sperry of Cranford and
Shelley Byron Hutchinson of Ypsilanti, Michigan.

The company once claimed that they distributed three times more stamps than the U.S. Postal Service. The number of copies of their catalog and redemption books ranked them among the most printed pieces in America. And unlike postage stamps, you could cash their stamps in for anything from luggage to a card table and chairs to a TV or even furniture.

But, how did Green Stamps work? How did Sperry and Hutchinson make any money?

Through grocery stores, gas stations, and other retail outlets, they created what we now call a rewards program.

They sold their stamps, certificates, and Saver Books (which held the stamps) to the retailers, who then would give a certain number of stamps to customers based on how much they spent. The person with the stamps would then look through the catalog, pick something out, and save their Green Stamps to get it.

S&H had about 600 stores across the country at its peak, with the closest one to my hometown being in Texarkana. You took your stamps to the store and used them like cash for your item.

Each Saver Book had 24 pages, and each page had 50 points to be filled. Green Stamps came in denominations worth 1, 10 and up, but each page had to be filled with stamps totaling 50 points.

My mom would cram the stamps in a drawer, and when the drawer got full we'd head to the Formica dinette table in the kitchen and begin to lick and stick the stamps into the books.

About two pages in, I'd had enough and would try and find reasons to get out of licking. My mom would say that I didn't have to do it, but when it came time to pick something out, I wouldn't be participating if I quit.

I hung in there, but that Green Stamp glue tasted terrible. I can taste them now just thinking about it.

Green Stamps were serious business. Families would save together to buy something they otherwise couldn't afford. My mom said she got herself a nice mixer with Green Stamps because she wouldn't have been able to save for one of that quality.

That's another thing I remember about the items you got with the stamps. They were all well made.

But, Green Stamps also caused friction. Like having a sizable sum of money in a family, not everyone agrees on how the stamps should be spent.

My father came home from work one day and told the story of a man he worked with. The man and his wife had gone back and forth over how they were going to use their stamps. Obviously, the topic had become heated and drug out. One day at work, the man opened his lunchbox and pulled out what he thought was a sandwich. It was a sandwich of sorts.

It was two pieces of bread with a book of Green Stamps between them.

Dad never said anything about the outcome of that, but I've always assumed that the wife spent the stamps on what she wanted.

Green Stamps also became part of our vernacular. We went to work to, "Bring home some Green Stamps," and CB radio users warned that, "Old Smokey was up ahead collecting Green Stamps."

S&H Green Stamps did have competitors, but they were never as popular. Gold Stamps and Plaid Stamps are ones that I recall, but there were others.

What is surprising is that Green Stamps are still around. Sort of.

In 2000, what was once S&H Green Stamps found itself facing what every other old business model faced: the Internet. That was the year that they made the move to the web.

The site greenpoints.com allows you to accrue points based on purchases from participating businesses. They even accept old S&H Green Stamps. However, you have to jump through hoops to cash them in. You have to send in a minimum of 26 books, be the original owner of the stamps, say where you got them, etc.

They aren't making it easy to use them. And, what you can get with them isn't very exciting. Mainly, it's gift cards for businesses and restaurants.

Today, grocery stores offer reward programs that allow you to buy discounted gasoline, but once upon a time, grocery stores gave Green Stamps. And those Green Stamps gave a 7-year-old boy and his sister a new swing set.

The Summer of '76

There was almost no breeze. Record temperatures were being shattered in England, and the southern U.S. was also pretty darn hot.

But three teenage kids in Arkansas decided that it would be a great idea to live in my backyard for most of the summer of 1976.

My cousin Randy was up from Alvin, Texas. I honestly can't remember why he stayed with us for so many weeks, but I do remember that my mom quickly reached the end of her rope in regard to a couple of rowdy boys in the house.

So, Randy and I went out and cranked open the pop-up camper. At first, we did it just to have a place to go to give my mom a break, but it became a brilliant idea.

My best friend Clint, who lived across the street and was a couple of years older than Randy and me, popped by. He loved our new "clubhouse," as he called it.

"Clubhouse?" I asked.

Clint pointed out that this was the perfect clubhouse for guys. We didn't have to construct anything, we had sleeping bunks and a stove, and we could run an extension cord from the back of my parents' house into the Coleman camper for lights and whatever else we needed that required electricity.

I ventured into the house to get my mother's permission for us to "get a couple of things" to take out to the camper for us to just hang out for the day. She happily agreed.

That day would last virtually all of America's Bicentennial summer.

You'd think that people would have had enough of silly love songs
I look around me and I see it isn't so
Some people want to fill the world with silly love songs
And what's wrong with that

Paul McCartney and Wings played often on the transistor radio we had imported into the camper.

We brought in a fan, an ice chest of soda pop, bags of chips, and other snack food. We also had several decks of cards.

45

We spent the day riding our bikes all over town. We would mow the occasional yard to raise the necessary funds for soda pop, chips, or a milkshake from Herb's Creamland, a hometown burger stand.

But after the sun would set, we headed to the camper. It would take a couple of hours for the temp to become bearable. We secured the window flaps open on the outside of the camper walls so that the night air could circulate through. We propelled the hot breeze from side to side with an old oscillating fan we'd borrowed from the house.

After getting some air moving, and some sodas and snacks out on the table, we played canasta. Canasta is a card game that is supposed to be played in teams. But, Clint's mom had showed him a variation that three people could play. We were competitive. It was a blast.

Just let your love flow
Like a mountain stream
And let your love grow
With the smallest of dreams
And let your love show
And you'll know what I mean
It's the season

The Bellamy Brothers came on the radio. We sang along, off-key, but with great enthusiasm.

We stayed up until all hours playing cards. We laughed, we told jokes, and we talked about the start of the school year and how it was looming. Clint was already in high school, I would be in my sophomore year, and Randy still had a year of junior high.

All alone at the end of the evening
And the bright lights have faded to blue.
I was thinking 'bout a woman who might have loved me
I never knew

The Eagles were on the verge of becoming one of the biggest recording acts in American history. They sang as we continued to enjoy our camper clubhouse.

Other than going into the house for showers, changes of clothes, or to eat nutritious meals that were mandated by my mother, Clint, Randy and I lived in that camper virtually all summer.

We just viewed it as a fun way to pass the school break. We had no inkling of the responsibilities that were just around the corner, or that this would be one of the last carefree summers of our lives.

Summer ended. We cleaned out the camper, put away the radio, the fan and the cards, and cranked the camper back down. Randy went home to Alvin, and Clint and I went back to school.

It has been said that youth is wasted on the young. I disagree. I believe teens deserve those carefree years. And I encourage them to use their summers to

47

bond, live life, and as the Eagles advised me 40 years ago, to "take it to the limit, one more time."

CHAPTER THREE – WHEN I WAS IN SCHOOL

The Chemistry Chicken

We had done the math, and without a doubt, Todd and I were going to flunk 11th grade chemistry.

It was 1978 and as my buddy and I sat in the back of Mr. Smith's room, we knew that we would run out of school year before we had any chance of making a passing grade.

We were desperate.

As class was dismissed, we waited until all of the other students left the room.

"Mr. Smith?" I said. "Can we talk to you for a second?"

"This wouldn't have anything to do with the fact that you boys are failing, would it?" Mr. Smith asked.

"Yes, sir," Todd said.

"Well, exactly what is it that you two think that I can do about that?" he said.

"In exchange for a passing grade, we are willing to offer our services for anything that would be helpful to you and the class," I said.

"Anything?" He said.

"Pretty much," said Todd.

"I want a chicken skeleton. In a nice glass case," said Mr. Smith.

Mr. Smith also taught a biology class and obviously needed a chicken skeleton.

Todd and I looked at each other, then back at him.

"You got it," Todd said.

We left.

"Where do you buy a chicken skeleton?" I asked my partner as we walked to our next class.

"I don't know," he said.

We both went home and asked our parents where to buy a chicken skeleton. My dad looked at me as if I had three eyes. He informed me that if I wanted a chicken skeleton, I needed to start with a live chicken.

I called Todd, and he said that his dad told him the same thing.

So, the next day, Todd and I bought a chicken from a local man.

As we drove back to Todd's house, I said, "So, do we shoot it or break its neck?"

"Can't do either," Todd said. "Can't break any of the bones if we're going to make a skeleton."

He had a point.

"I guess we have to smother it," I said.

"I guess so," he said.

We arrived at Todd's house and took the chicken and the cage out of the car.

We both stared at the chicken.

"Well," I said. "You wanna hold or smother?"

"I'll smother," he said.

I'll spare you the next 10 minutes of the story, but suffice it to say, chickens are a lot like people. They don't like to be smothered.

At first, we decided to pluck the chicken, but then our hands got tired, so we took him and, feathers and all, threw him in a boiling pot in Todd's mom's kitchen.

There's a reason that a chicken's insides are removed before they're boiled. About 15 minutes into the boiling process, the smell began to be annoying. Then it became unbearable.

We opened the windows and turned on the fans.

It still smelled awful.

About this time, Todd's mom came home. Boy, was she mad.

Todd, myself and the boiled chicken all found ourselves in the front yard. We dumped out everything in the yard and slowly went through it.

This was way before the Internet, so we had to look through the encyclopedia to find a photo and bone count of a chicken.

Once we found all of the bones, we proceeded to clean and dry them. Using the picture in the "Funk & Wagnalls," we used glue and coat hangers to build our chicken skeleton on a wooden base.

The hardware store had the wood and glass for the rest of the display case.
When we took the chicken skeleton to Mr. Smith, we could tell that he was impressed.

"You boys have a much brighter future in chicken skeletons than you do in chemistry," he said.

Todd and I got our passing grades, went on to the 12th grade, graduation, and then on with our lives.

Several years after graduation, I returned to my old high school for an event.

When it was over, I was walking back to the parking lot and passed my old chemistry classroom. I stopped and peered through the window.

There it was. Right where it sat the last time I saw it. Sitting on a table near the front of the classroom.

The chemistry chicken had not died in vain.

Tick Tock

I read something recently that was a bit disconcerting. Someone was offering a class to teach children how to tell time.

Think about that.

We've simplified the most basic things to the point where children – the very group of people that we will all rely on to run the country and take care of running things, such as our nursing homes when we reach old age – can't read a watch or a clock.

Sure, kids, or anyone else for that matter, can look at a cell phone or a digital device and know what time it is. But, they can't read the face of an analog clock.

On the surface, this may seem like no big deal, but this is the latest in a trend of basics that someone, somewhere along the way, decided wasn't important enough for our children to learn.

Children are not being taught the most rudimentary of abilities that we all learned and take for granted.

A few years ago, I heard that cursive writing was no longer being taught in schools. I suspected (incorrectly, it seems) that maybe that was a voluntary thing. Now, I'm hearing that kids are being dinged or chastised for using cursive.

My generation was taught typing. That is now called keyboarding. Don't get me wrong, typing is one of the most valuable skill sets I acquired in high school. For young people now, that's no different. But, what happens when the electricity goes off?

There's nothing wrong with printing as a form of writing, but cursive is a much faster means of communication. I can remember spending hours in third and fourth grade practicing cursive. I was never very good at it, and I'm still not, but cursive used to be an art form.

Look at the United States Constitution and the Declaration of Independence. James Madison and Thomas Jefferson, respectively, painstakingly used a quill pen and ink to write out, in cursive, what are two of the most important documents that history has ever seen.

Good penmanship used to be a point of pride, and it was often beautiful.

Computers have not only all but eliminated handwriting from our kids' list of abilities, they've also all but omitted the need to go to the library. The hours that my age group spent learning the Dewey Decimal System as a pathway to research and expanding our knowledge has been replaced by websites that may or may not be reliable sources of information.

A few years ago, I went to our local book repository to sign my wife and myself up for library cards, and even donated some books while I was there. Each time I've visited since, the youngest person there was the lady working the counter.

Young people aren't learning how to find their own information. They rely almost solely on an electronic device and Google. I'm guessing that if you asked someone under age 30 if they could tell you about Funk & Wagnalls, they'd probably guess they were a Hip Hop group.

Reading a map is also being lost to time. It wasn't so long ago that a trip of any length first required stopping at a Texaco or Shell station to buy road maps or a road atlas of the states that connected you to your destination. Now, people blindly trust some unseen lady named Siri, who lives inside our cellphones to tell us where to go, turn and stop.

These same electronic devices have also essentially crippled us, should we actually have to remember someone's phone number. Keeping an address book (in pencil) was once standard in every household. We referenced them for numbers we called infrequently, but most people we called often required us to remember their numbers.

Today, young and old alike simply have to touch the name of the person we want to call on our cell, and we no longer learn or we have forgotten their actual number.

We have arrived at a place that is somewhat frightening. Fewer of us know how to do for ourselves. We blindly rely on a system of communication and information that, should someone flip off its switch tomorrow, most of us not only have no backup system, we wouldn't know how to use it if we did.

The best favor that we can do for younger people is to show them some basics. That is, before they no longer are willing to still listen and learn.

Yes, You Can Go Home Again

I vividly remember the night of my high school graduation. It was very hot and very wet.

Because of heavy rains, we were the first class in no-one-could-remember-how-long to graduate inside the gymnasium instead of on the football field.

It was a Friday night in May, and polyester was still surviving from the 1970s in the form of our shiny, purple caps and gowns.

As we all sat inside this metal building with no air conditioning, I began to count the number of sweat beads dripping from my face. That was preferable to listening to the drone of the speaker (I can't even remember now who it was) telling us that whatever lay ahead of us, we could rise above it.

At that moment, all I wanted to raise was a glass full of beer to toast my classmates and then move on with my life.

The ceremony eventually ended and we tossed our caps into the air. We hugged, took a few photos, and I darted for the door and my '72 Olds Cutlass in the parking lot.

I went home and showered and then we all met up at a predetermined place, far away from the grownups. We laughed, partied, enjoyed our evening, and then we all said goodbye.

That was 35 years ago.

Recently, it must've dawned on one of us that our 35th graduation anniversary was here.

Facebook, which no one could've ever dreamed of when we were in school, was an invaluable tool in finding many of my classmates. The call went out for all of us to gather for the homecoming game in our hometown. We'd all attend the game, and then gather the next night at a predetermined party spot, far away from the grownups.

I rolled into town, this time in a Prius instead of a much-cooler '72 Olds Cutlass, and of course, it was raining.

My friend Kirk is now an elected official, a city treasurer of all things, and was in charge of cooking the hamburgers for the booster club at the homecoming game. I offered to help.

As I walked toward the football stadium down the same sidewalk, in front of the same high school gymnasium where I'd graduated 3 1/2 decades earlier, I thought about how ironic it was that rain had sent us on our way so many years before, and now it seemed to be welcoming us back home.

I also thought about the fact that the same guy I was in math class with was somehow now counting money for a living.

A handful actually made it to the game. We stood under the pavilion, moving from one side to the other trying to simultaneously dodge the rain and the smoke from the hamburger grill.

I ran into a number of people from my past, asked about others, and met the children of some of my classmates. Most of their children are older now than we were when we graduated.

The next evening, we gathered at a classmate's home. And, I'll be honest, there were lots of folks walking up the driveway that I didn't recognize. I would turn and say, "Help me out, here. Who is that?" But I wasn't the only one doing it. The fact is that 35 years changes most folks.

Only a handful looked close to what they did back in the day, and they were all told as much.

Everyone brought a dish, and we ate, had a few cocktails, and visited until well after dark. It really was a fun time.

There is a comfort level that you have with your schoolmates that never goes away. Time, distance, and other factors may place us in completely different worlds from each other, but no matter how long you've been apart, seeing each other again brings back a kinship that can't be erased.

As the rain continued, we hugged, took a few photos, and I darted for the door and my 2008 Prius in the parking area.

As I drove home, I thought about how long 35 years is. And, how seeing everyone again made it seem not that long at all.

CHAPTER FOUR – HOME FOR THE HOLIDAYS

Let Us Give Thanks

Our major holidays are centered around faith. Easter, Hanukkah, and Christmas focus on God. So does Thanksgiving, but it focuses on appreciating what the other holidays represent.

My earliest memories of Thanksgiving are of my sister and me riding in the back seat of my mom's 1960 model Buick and traveling from one grandparent's house to the other. I was very fortunate as a child. Virtually all members of both sides of my family lived in the same town.

Ashdown, Arkansas, was and still is a small town. So, it was easy to make your way to multiple stops on a Thanksgiving Day.

Alternating between locations for dinner and supper (in the South, we call it dinner and supper, not lunch and dinner), we would go to my mom's parents' house and then my dad's parents', or vise versa, and visit and eat.

I can still see the men and boys sitting in the living room watching a snowy, black and white picture of the football game. I can hear my grandfather, dad and uncles yelling at the screen. Tom Landry is pacing the sideline in his trademark suit, tie and fedora.

The women and girls are laughing in the kitchen and talking about what recipe each will make when we are all back together at Christmas.

We get the call from our grandmother that the food is ready. We rise, bow our heads, and my grandfather leads us in prayer, thanking God for everything.

The adults gather around the table and the kids fix our own plates. We are relegated to a card table in the living room.

Dessert is next. When the kids are invited back to the kitchen, the dishes and glasses have been cleaned up and the table is now full of pies, cakes, brownies and other sweets. I look until I spot the pecan and chocolate pies. Both of my grandmothers made amazing pecan pie, and my mom always made a wonderful chocolate.

After dessert, the adults have coffee and the children are sent outside to play. One of the great things about having a lot of cousins is that you can field your own sports team. We toss the football and run through the cold, autumn air. Our noses turn red and our eyes water. We laugh and laugh some more.

At the end of a long day of visiting, we all part ways and head back to our respective homes. With leftovers that our grandmothers have put together for each family, we will enjoy turkey, ham, dressing and other side dishes for days.

I make sure my mom also brings plenty of pecan and chocolate pie.

Faster and faster, the calendar begins to flip. Each passing year sees more empty chairs at the kitchen table. Suddenly, one year, I'm invited to sit at the table with the adults. My children now are the ones at the card table in the living room, and Tom Landry no longer walks the sideline.

More time passes, and my grandchildren now sit at the card table.

Life is short. Thanksgiving is an annual reminder of that. It is a time of joy, but it is also a time for reflection.

God gives us all many blessings. Thanksgiving is the marker on the highway of life that reminds us our lives and ultimate destination are all part of one, big blessing. A reminder for which we each need to be thankful. Not just on a holiday, but every day.

The Evel Knievel Super Stunt Cycle with Gyro Launcher

All I wanted for Christmas was an Evel Knievel Super Stunt Cycle with Gyro Launcher.

In 1973, every eleven-year-old boy in America wanted to be Evel Knievel.

Moms in 1970s America worried about a lot – but if they had a son between the ages of 8 and 18, they worried about Evel Knievel.

Mr. Knievel made his living wearing a skintight American-themed jumpsuit and cape while driving a motorcycle 100 miles per hour and jumping over buses, cars or anything else he liked.

The Evel Knievel Super Stunt Cycle toy had a hand crank, which you wound quickly to get the back wheel of the motorcycle spinning. With a quick stop of the handle, you would launch it. The Knievel bike and doll would scream away and over a ramp.

I waited months for Christmas and that toy to arrive.

Sure enough, on Christmas Eve (Santa visited us on Christmas Eve, not morning) as my parents led us into the living room, there it was under the tree. I was beyond excited.

But, wait. "Too dark to play with that now. Wait until morning," they said.

I was awake most of the night thinking of the impressive stunts I'd do the next morning.

Finally, sunrise.

As the rest of my family still slept, I threw on my robe, grabbed my stunt cycle and made my way outside with my dream toy.

I loaded it, cranked it, and launched it.

And it broke on the very first launch.

The bike landed on its back instead of the wheels and pieces flew everywhere when it hit the concrete.

I sat and stared in disbelief. Evel was down and he wasn't getting back up.

It was 1973 and there was no Super Glue.

With my dreams shattered, I spent the rest of the holiday and most of 1974 brooding over my loss.

But the years that have passed have given me perspective. I have learned that there are much more important things in life than toys.

Technology, for example. Like eBay. Where I found an Evel Knievel Super Stunt Cycle with Gyro Launcher, mint in the box.

It should be here by Christmas.

Christmas Traditions: Presents, Pictures and Pangburn's

Santa came to our house on Christmas Eve, before we went to bed. Some of my friends had to go to bed before Santa would come. Their gifts would be under the tree when they woke up.

Not me. I didn't have to wait. My grandmother would take us for a Christmas Eve ride in the station wagon to look for Rudolph's glowing nose in the sky.

All of the local radio stations would give Santa sighting reports. The North American Aerospace Defense Command (NORAD) would provide constant updates. The radio announcer passed those along as my sister and I would press our noses to the window and look for Rudolph's glow. I would instruct her to look through the window on the other side of the car. That way, one of us could alert the other if he was spotted.

Somehow, while my sister and I were cruising in the Ford Country Squire, Santa and his sleigh team would have landed on the roof of our house on Beech Street, he would have slid down the chimney and left our gifts while we were out.

Dad would always shrug and tell us that we had "just missed him."

My sister and I had seen Santa and talked to him at Sears and Roebuck, and we even had our picture made with him. But, I wanted to see him again on Christmas Eve. My sister was a little more wary of Saint Nick. The pictures taken at Sears reflect that.

After arriving back home to the toys and gifts under the tree, Perry Como, Andy Williams, Dean Martin, Bing Crosby and Nat King Cole would sing.

Sometimes, we would listen to them sing on the radio, other times they would be on the television.

ABC, NBC and CBS would all put the stars on for Christmas specials. Bob Hope was frequently there. The black-and-white TV would play in the background. Sometimes the picture was clear, other times it was snowy.

Our stockings, which had been hung by the chimney with care, were loaded with walnuts, oranges, apples and small gifts. There were spinning tops, marbles and jacks.

One year, I was overjoyed to receive cap guns, complete with plenty of boxes of long, red ammo strips. This meant that playing cowboys and Indians was on tap for the coming days.

While we celebrated, my dad would drink Folgers from the percolator in the kitchen. We would raid the newly opened box of Pangburn's Chocolate.

After we had opened our presents, my mom would have us pose for pictures. She always had us sit on the fireplace hearth and hold some of our gifts for the picture taking. The fireplace photos were first taken when we were quite small, and my mom would take them each year until we left home. Those photos now reside in a Pangburn's Chocolate box.

Later, I would continue the Christmas Eve tradition with my own children. Santa would arrive before bedtime, allowing for presents, pictures and Pangburn's.

We would take their photos with them holding some of their gifts. Bing Crosby and Nat King Cole would sing from the CD player. The TV networks aired Christmas specials, which included the stars of the day. All were things that we continued until they left home.

Christmas traditions vary from family to family, but it's these traditions that are the common thread that connects generations.

Jesus is the reason for the season, but the joy the season brings to children is one of the best feelings there is. We should never lose focus of why we celebrate Christmas, but we also shouldn't lose the opportunity to hand down the things that made our Christmases memorable to our children, grandchildren and beyond.

And we should all take a moment each year to dig out that Pangburn's box and say hello to everyone from Christmases past. Including those who drove us around in a station wagon on Christmas Eve while Santa slid down the chimney.

CHAPTER FIVE – FOOD AND BEVERAGES

Fried Baloney Sandwiches

Peanut butter and jelly sandwiches were a mainstay of a '70s kid's childhood and they've hung around. But, what happened to fried baloney sandwiches?

Unlike many of today's kids, who play video games most of the day, a typical morning for kids in my neighborhood would see a mom sending you out the back door with a pat on the rear and a "Don't be late for lunch" warning.

After coming in from a hard three or four hours of playing baseball on the corner lot, a fried baloney sandwich on white bread with Miracle Whip and a plate full of Fritos would always hit the spot.

I was 26 before I found out that baloney wasn't a food group.

At my house, I was the designated baloney fetcher. When we would run low, mom would say "Johnny, go down to Shur Way and get Mr. Pope to slice us up a pound of baloney. And ask him to put it on our ticket."

Back in those days, baloney came in large slabs and could be sliced to the thickness of your choice. Also, people trusted you to pay your bills. Your 10-year-old kid could charge baloney and Fritos, no questions asked.

I would gladly hop on my purple Murray bike, with the banana seat and the sissy bar, and peddle my way to the store. I'd pass all of the pop bottles out back behind Shur Way, which were waiting to be picked up by the soda pop truck driver. I'd come to a gliding stop up onto the sidewalk, lean my bike up against the side of the store, and make my way to the front.

As I entered through the glass door, which had a "C'mon in, it's KOOL inside" sticker by the handle, I'd pass the cartons of cigarettes and slowly begin to soak up the air conditioning on my way to the meat counter in the back. The Popes were great people and had a reputation for really good meat products. The front of the store assured you of that with an "Our Meats Are Better" sign.

And they were.

Mr. Pope would take my baloney order, one or two pounds, and I'd stand there covered in sand and sweat and watch as he'd throw the baloney slab onto the slicer. Like an artisan, he'd have that baloney sliced, wrapped in butcher paper, taped shut and in my hand in no time at all. He'd pull the pencil from behind his ear and mark the price on the paper.

I'd sign the ticket, hop on my bike and head back down Beech Street, baloney in tow.

Mom always used the same cast iron skillet to fry baloney. She knew how to cook it to that perfection of blackness that was absolutely delicious.

There were other foods that were staples, including wienies and kraut. My little sister couldn't say "wienies and kraut." She pronounced it "wienies and crap," which I think was more accurate. We ate whatever mom fixed, but fried baloney sandwiches were my favorite.

Shur Way is gone now. So is Mr. Pope. But mom gave me her skillet and there's one or two real meat markets still open near where I live.

I think today I'll give the family a treat and do the cooking.

I no longer have my purple Murray bike, but I do have a pickup truck and a hankering for a fried baloney sandwich.

Tastee Freez and the A&W

My earliest recollection of hamburgers were ground beef patties that my mom fried in a cast iron skillet and placed between two pieces of white bread that were coated in Miracle Whip.

I'm sure that the burgers were fried in bacon drippings that had been saved from breakfast, because virtually everything we ate back then was fried in bacon drippings that had been saved from breakfast.

As I got older and my parents felt that I was suitable to take out in public, we'd go out to eat on Friday nights. Many times, it was to go get a hamburger and French fries.

My hometown of Ashdown, Arkansas, had about 3,000 people in those days, so there was no McDonald's, Burger King or Wendy's.

If you wanted a burger, you had a few options, but I always liked it when we went to the Tastee Freez.

Tastee Freez was a good place to eat, and they had 100 different flavors of milkshakes. The coconut-flavored milkshake was my favorite. From burritos to burgers, they had it all.

I can remember sitting in a booth munching on a burger. I'd watch out the window as the teenage guys would drive up in a Chevelle, Camaro, Mustang or Firebird and flirt with the girls.

John Mellencamp would later immortalize the Tastee Freez in his song "Jack and Diane."

Unfortunately, the Tastee Freez has gone the way of the Chevelle and the Firebird. A Google search showed that they're still around, but found primarily in California – and even Alaska, of all places. You'd think that people in Alaska were already cold enough without a Tastee Freez.

Sometimes, we'd go to Texarkana to the A&W Root Beer drive-in. To this day I've never had a better root beer than an A&W served in one of their frosty mugs.

In the '60s, A&W had a brilliant marketing campaign. They'd give each kid under about age 10 a tiny A&W root beer mug with their logo on it, and offer kids free root beer if accompanied by a parent. The mug seemed huge to me at the time. My mom kept my A&W mug, and a few years ago she showed it to me. I've seen shot glasses bigger than that thing.

I remember A&W had hamburgers, but I'm afraid they were overshadowed in my mind by the free root beer.

A&W stands are also still around according to Google, but not anywhere close to where I live.

The best hamburger I find these days is one that I discovered after moving to Texas.

Whataburger.

I know that there are those who will argue that there are better burgers than a Whataburger, but I would argue that those folks are simply misguided.

If you ever want to know if a Whataburger all-the-way with cheese isn't the best burger you've ever eaten, I dare you to move someplace where they have no Whataburgers.

Or, just on a trial basis, stay somewhere for a month where there are no Whataburgers. I have friends who've left the Lone Star State, and the first thing they want to do when they come back to visit is go to Whataburger.

My point of all of this is that somewhere along the way, we lost the Tastee Freez and A&W, so let's all band together and do whatever we can to make sure we don't lose Whataburger.

Maybe we can get John Mellencamp to write a song about it.

Chocolate Gravy

You haven't lived until you've had chocolate gravy.

Whenever some chef comes on television and demonstrates a 40-step process for the "perfect meal," I wonder how we got so far away from biscuits and gravy. Specifically, biscuits and chocolate gravy.

Being a Southern boy, I was lucky enough to be reared on the staples of poor folk food. Of course, I had no idea that what we were eating was poor folk food.

I just knew that it tasted like a million dollars and assumed that everyone's parents fed them meals that were built on the Southern Food Pyramid: beef, potatoes, flour and bacon grease.

In the '60s, many World War II and Korean veterans were raising their families on one salary. It was a priority for a mom to be at home raising the kiddos, so a dollar was stretched as far as it could go.

This meant that every single food item was made to taste as good as possible and last as long as possible. Back then, no one had ever heard about cholesterol.

Shockingly, we were surrounded by skinny people who died of old age.

When I was a lad, EVERY meal had the following: homemade biscuits, gravy and fried potatoes. This was at breakfast, lunch and dinner. No exceptions.

On special occasions, my mom made chocolate gravy for breakfast.

Now, before you turn up your nose and get all holier-than-thou, let me just tell you that people came from miles around for my mom's chocolate gravy. Every time I had buddies spend the weekend, they requested it.

But, chocolate gravy is not what you think. It's not really a gravy so much as it's a dessert.

My Great Aunt Maude gets the credit for this dish. My mother tells stories about how she and her five siblings would visit Aunt Maude and looked forward to chocolate gravy.

Chocolate gravy is more like a hot pudding, but it has the consistency of gravy. Hence the name.

I share this with you in the hopes that you will try it, like it, feed it to your kids, they will like it and then chocolate gravy will live on.

Chocolate Gravy

1 cup of sugar

4 tablespoons of cocoa

1 teaspoon of self-rising flour

1/4 cup of butter

1 cup of milk

1/4 teaspoon of vanilla (optional)

Directions :
Mix sugar, flour & cocoa together, well.

Then add milk, butter & vanilla.

Bring to a boil. Reduce heat & cook on low until done to preferred consistency. Pour over hot, buttered biscuits (split in half) and eat with a fork.

Velveeta, Ripple and Steve

I miss the days of Velveeta and ripple.

As a younger man, I considered myself a connoisseur of the finer things in life. Used Oldsmobiles, girls who parted their hair like Farrah Fawcett, and the occasional adult beverage.

By occasional, I mean any occasion.

The late 1970s were about as much like "That '70s Show" as the '50s were like "Happy Days." However, in the midst of all the manufactured nostalgia, what these two shows portrayed had a grain of truth to it.

We drank a lot of beer back then. The drinking age was 18, so it was legal to buy it. We all worked low-paying jobs and couldn't afford the good beer, so a purchase was based on an economical, dollar-to-quantity ratio rather than quality.

Seeing that I was obviously on a path to a yet-to-be-thought-of Jeff Foxworthy joke, my friend Steve decided to introduce me to some culture. He invited me to the Shakespeare Festival of Dallas in Fair Park.

At first I balked. I'd read Shakespeare and wasn't impressed. To me, a "Hamlet" should be a menu item at Denny's, not some play that you sit through in the middle of an amphitheater during a Texas August. However, after convincing me that I'd enjoy it and the price was right (free), I agreed.

We checked into our rooms near the park and Steve announced we'd now shop for wine and cheese. "Wine and cheese?" I asked. "Let's splurge on good beer," I added. Steve shook his head and said that he was making the call and that wine and cheese it would be.

As Steve shopped in one end of the store, I browsed the other. He found a bottle that cost $10 (a princely sum back then) and a block of Gouda. I'd never heard of either, but I had heard of Velveeta and ripple. The price seemed right on my find and we could get a whole lot more of both. Besides, I argued, if we left the Velveeta out in a bowl in the heat, we could bring a bag of chips and have dip, too.

Steve again shook his head, so wine and cheese it was.

We took our place in the audience and saw "As You Like It" with Sigourney Weaver in the role of Rosalind. For this kid who'd never seen real culture, my eyes were opened. I began to appreciate what I was experiencing. All of it. Classic literature came to life on stage, real actors, real wine and real cheese. It was amazing.

A news story regarding a Velveeta shortage made me think of all this. The Shakespeare, the wine, the cheese and Steve. Steve gave me an appreciation for a lot of things. He is the one who gave me my love of puns.

Steve died several years ago, and I miss him.

I think I'll buy some Velveeta before it's all gone and toast Steve with a glass of ripple. He wouldn't find the gesture classy, but he'd think it was a really Gouda idea.

Diners and Drive-ins are a Dying Breed

Chain restaurants are rapidly replacing what I believe has been one of the best facets of small town America: the local diner or restaurant.

Unexpectedly and unannounced, the drive-in in our small town closed last week. In fairness, it was a Sonic, which technically is a chain restaurant, but it wasn't a corporate location, it was locally owned.

Whenever we lose an eatery that was owned by someone who lives in our town, we lose a little bit of who we are.

After I learned that Sonic had closed its doors, I regretted not making the drive to it more often for a

Number 3 with cheese, some onion rings, and a limeade.

In my hometown, Sonic was one of the first chain restaurants to open a location there. We also got a Pizza Hut. We thought that was pretty exciting stuff in the 1970s; but then again, we were also the same bunch who thought it was a major event when we got a traffic light to replace the flashing red one at the main four-way-stop.

The Sonic and Pizza Hut never supplanted our home-owned eateries. There was enough business for everyone.

But one thing is certain. It was never the Sonic or the Pizza Hut that were the culinary identity of our little town. From the 1960s through the 1980s, Mac's Cafe, Mesamore's Restaurant, and Herb's Creamland were the main eateries for which Ashdown, Arkansas, was best known. Today, only Herb's remains.

Mac's began in a small building in Ogden, Arkansas. I don't know if it opened in the '50s or '60s, but I vaguely remember it moving the seven miles or so north to Ashdown on Highway 71.

Every restaurant had its signature dish, and for me, it was Mac's hot steak sandwich. Why it was called a sandwich, I don't know, because it wasn't. It was a chicken fried steak, smothered with gravy. The sides were fries and a salad, with a piece of white bread toast, cut diagonally and placed on either side of the plate.

I loved Mac's salad dressing on crackers, and would eat that while waiting on my food order. I'm pretty sure that the salad dressing was mayonnaise and ketchup, mixed together with spices.

Mac's sat next to a truck stop, so many of the men who sat on the bar stools at the counter were driving through. As I would eat at my booth or table in the dining room, I watched them guzzle coffee, chain smoke, and hit on the waitresses. The jukebox would repeat the same Merle Haggard and Loretta Lynn songs.

Mac's was comfortable. It was part of who we all were.

Mesamore's Restaurant was our nice, sit-down eatery. It had a meeting room for the local civic groups' luncheons. The fare at Mesamore's was more like a traditional menu. Fish, steaks and chops were available.

Herb's Creamland, later just called Herb's, began as a tiny stand on the side of the highway. Opened in 1954, Herb's was and still is a mainstay in Ashdown. A trip through my hometown isn't complete without a Herb Burger and a basket of fries. I know that it has been in business at four different locations over the years. It was the hangout for all of us from the time I was about 12 until I moved away after high school.

Herb was my cousin. We lost him a few years ago.

Tyler and East Texas have been my adopted home for years. I moved here in February 1987. The kind folks here welcomed me with open arms, but one of the best favors they did for me was to introduce me to the best local eateries.

Some are now gone, but a handful remain. Fuller's Fine Foods, which was located on Front Street, is now an empty lot. Other favorites over the years have included D's Coffee Shop and Cox's Grill.

Hands down, my favorite of the remaining old-school restaurants in Tyler is Loggin's. Located on Glenwood, Loggin's began in the 1940s as a drive-in. Now, it offers a daily lunch buffet with all of the dishes that remind me a lot of Mac's Cafe.

Chicken-fried steak, mashed potatoes and gravy, catfish, and some of the best pie you'll ever eat, is just the beginning of what you'll find. When strawberries are in season, try the strawberry cobbler. It's amazing.

Eating out is a treat. But the next time you do, consider supporting the locally owned eateries. They truly are part of who we are and what makes our towns great. And I'd like to see them stay around for generations to come.

Going Dutch

A number of years ago, I stumbled across a television program on what was then a new cable offering called the RFD-TV channel. A man named Cee Dub was on the screen cooking an entire meal using only Dutch ovens. I was fascinated.

I vaguely remembered these cast iron pots with three legs from my days in the Scouts. I made it through Cub Scouts and Webelos, but only a year or so of Boy Scouts. By about age 12, I left the Boy Scouts for sports and other endeavors.

I suspect that the use of Dutch ovens and fire probably was entrusted more to the older boys, which, with my departure from the Boy Scouts of America, would explain my lack of familiarity with the use of these historic and still viable cooking vessels.

Back to Cee Dub. I set the DVR to record his upcoming shows. As I watched more episodes, I learned that he was a retired game warden from the state of Idaho who had parlayed his assignment as camp cook during his working years into a television program, cookbooks and weekend camp retreats, to teach others how to cook the way of the American pioneers and cowboys.

What fascinated me about Dutch oven cooking was that anything you can cook in a regular oven can be cooked in a Dutch oven. You can also boil or fry food in them.

From a pot roast to a chicken to a casserole to a peach cobbler to biscuits, if you follow the right heat formula above and beneath your pot, you can cook a gourmet meal in the woods or on your back porch.

Here's a little history about Dutch ovens. My search to find out why they're named what they are led to no definitive answer. Some believe that it has to do with the Dutch figuring out a better manufacturing process for the ovens. Others believe they got their name from the Dutch settlers in America. No one seems to know for sure.

One thing that isn't in doubt is the versatility and value these pots have possessed through the years. One story tells of George Washington's mother leaving half of what was referred to as her "iron kitchen furniture" to a grandson, and the other half to a granddaughter. That was in 1788.

The early settlers in this country relied on Dutch ovens for cooking virtually every meal. The cast iron evenly distributed heat, and the lids provided a way to add the right amount of warmth to the top of what was being cooked.

As the country expanded west, cowboys and chuckwagon cooks relied on Dutch ovens for the long rides and keeping cowpokes fed.

Most of the Dutch ovens that are popular today are similar to what the cowboys used. They're referred to as "cowboy," "chuckwagon," or "camp" Dutch ovens. They have three short legs and a lid with a lip around it.

Since heat rises, you need fewer hot coals under the oven than you do on the top. The art of cooking with these ovens is knowing how many coals to keep underneath and on top. Factors such as size of the coals and wind can cause temp spikes. Ignoring your coals can cause temp drops. You really do have to practice.

One of the best litmus tests for the progress you're making on the dish your cooking is something that Cee Dub often says on his show. "If it smells done, it's done. If it smells burnt, it's burnt."

He's right.

My first foray into giving this type of cooking a shot was using a Lodge 10-inch Dutch oven my friend George gave me. He surprised me with this gift after I mentioned I'd been watching the TV show and was going to give this new hobby a try. Lodge and Camp Chef are the primary manufactures of the better ovens. Cheaper ones are available, but I wouldn't recommend them.

I kept my first dish simple. It was a can of Pillsbury Flaky Biscuits. I used charcoal briquettes as my heat source and they came out great.

From there, I've added larger ovens to my collection and cooked roasts, vegetables and desserts. You can also stack Dutch ovens, with the largest on the bottom to the smallest one on the top. This allows you to utilize all of the heat to its maximum potential.

Truly, anything you can cook in the oven in your house, you can cook in a Dutch oven.

I've also discovered another heat source for Dutch ovens instead of fire and coals: a solar oven.

Solar ovens are simple. They're a box with four reflecting panels that direct the sun's rays into the box chamber. You can place a smaller Dutch oven inside the solar oven and use the free energy to cook your meal.

Both Dutch and solar ovens are a lot of fun, especially for children, who often have little idea how food is cooked. Exposing kids, or even adults, to this type of outdoor cooking often turns into a fun hobby between friends. There are many groups who spend time camping and having friendly cooking competitions. Roaming from campsite to campsite and sampling the different dishes is common.

Not only is cooking outdoors fun, it is also a good backup way that you can prepare food during a power outage or disaster.

After I finish writing this, I plan on making some baked potatoes in one of my prized three-legged, cast iron vessels. My wife is out of town at the moment and a buddy of mine is coming over.

For this lunch, we're going Dutch.

Chewing the Fat

Some men do things they aren't supposed to when their wife leaves town. I'm no exception.

I kissed her goodbye and told her that I loved her, I would miss her, and to tell her mother hello. The first chance I got after her departure, I did a rapid, cursory inspection of the refrigerator.

Just as I suspected. It was full of healthy food.

I toppled the stacks of fat-free yogurt as I parted them like the Red Sea, looking for something that didn't taste like a bland Elmer's Glue. People who make yogurt think that if they give it a fancy-sounding Greek name and some colorful graphics, that we won't notice that it tastes like paste.

The yogurt people claim right there on the plastic tub that "Nostimo" means "delicious." But, I spent many an hour in the third grade trying to impress the girls with my glue-eating abilities, so they aren't fooling me one bit. I know Elmer's Glue Lite when I taste it.

After removing the alleged yogurt from the fridge and restacking it on the kitchen counter, I run into my next healthy obstacle: a rotisserie chicken. I'd highly doubt that Colonel Harland Sanders ever ate a rotisserie chicken, much less considered selling one. He built a chicken empire on fried chicken, not rotisserie chicken.

Now, there'll be plenty of folks who would say that Kentucky Fried Chicken isn't good for you, and they'd be right. It finally killed Colonel Sanders when he was 90.

I placed the rotisserie chicken on the counter next to the Greek yogurt, and continued my search. Behind the chicken was lite sour cream, lite cream cheese, lite cheese, and a light. The one that goes off when you shut the refrigerator door. Which is what I did.

It was time to go to the store.

I entered the store and was greeted by a display with heat lamps that were keeping beef and pork ribs warm. To the right was a tall display of Krispy Kreme Donuts. Glazed, chocolate-covered, and cake donuts.

I've never cheated on my wife, but I was pretty sure that ogling a dozen Krispy Kremes was fairly close to what that feels like.

I pushed the buggy passed the ribs and donuts, hung a left at the imported beer, and there it was: the meat counter.

I slowly guided the buggy past the peppered bacon, spicy sausage, bratwurst, and had just begun to make my way through the lunch meats and refrigerated pickles, when I caught her out of the corner of my eye. The butcher was gently placing briskets in a neat row.

When she put the last one out on the stack, she tweaked the sign with the sale price to make sure that I could see it. She smiled at me, wiped her hands on her apron, and pushed the squeaky metal cart between the saloon-style doors before disappearing, leaving the brisket and me to talk amongst ourselves.

"Hello, there," I said to the brisket. "Any plans for the weekend?"

I picked up the last one she had placed on the stack, put it in the buggy, and moved on to the beef kabobs.

Let me tell you, whoever thought of making kabobs that are ready to go on the grill is a genius. I rank them right up there with whoever invented the TV remote and the wheel.

A couple of kabob packages joined the brisket in the basket, and I then rolled on to the section with the Angus hamburger patties. Three packages of those joined the brisket and the kabobs, and I was ready to check out.

"Lots of company this weekend?" the cashier asked me. Not wanting to be dishonest, I answered her.

"Lots," I said with a convincing nod.

When I got home, the cat watched me unload my haul. She gave me the look that said, "I'm going to tell Mom."

On the back porch, I fired up the Big Green Egg (a large, ceramic smoker) with a stack of lump charcoal in the bottom, and placed the brisket on 250. "I'll see you in the morning," I said to the brisket.

After making my way to the Man Cave, I lit the gas grill and lined the grate with hamburger patties and kabobs. The meat began to sizzle just as the sun set and a cold rain began to fall.

I built a fire in the wood stove. The heat was just enough to keep the Man Cave warm, with the open doors allowing the smell of the rain to complement the beef's aroma.

As the rain faded, the kabobs and burgers were done. I piled them into Pyrex dishes and made my way to the house.

A kabob and a burger filled my plate. I thought about the mountain men I see on TV and how they go out into the rain and darkness to forage and cook their food. Just like me.

The next morning, the brisket had a perfect smoke ring around it, and the internal temp was just right. I slid the brisket from the Big Green Egg onto a broiler pan and took it into the kitchen.

I sliced it into sections and placed them in Ziploc bags. The brisket, and the leftover kabobs and burgers are now hidden in the back of the freezer.

Just to make sure I'm not found out, I paid the cat off with chunks of rotisserie chicken, and I used some of the Greek yogurt to repair a couple of picture frames.

CHAPTER SIX – RADIO AND RECORDS

Listening With Frequency

In 1972, when I was 10 years old, my dad's parents gave me a Christmas present that would change my life: a Sony ICR-1826 model transistor radio.

This small, white cube would send me down a career path that only a lucky few travel.

Late at night, long after I was supposed to have been asleep, I would turn the radio down low next to my pillow and tune in voices from hundreds, or even thousands, of miles away.

The voices came from Dallas, Chicago, Nashville, Denver and San Antonio. I was amazed. This tiny, battery-powered box could harvest my choice of entertainment with the turn of a dial.

I'd lie awake in the dark and listen to the announcers carry on a conversation with me without me saying a word. They'd talk over the music and somehow magically stop talking just as the singer came in.

They'd tell me what was happening in the world. They'd promise me that the next big hit song would be heard on their station first.

I couldn't get enough of it.

I became fascinated with the medium called radio.

Coincidentally, that same year, my hometown of Ashdown, Arkansas, got its own radio station.

Unfortunately, my new radio was AM only. The new radio station was on the FM dial. No problem. My parents' console stereo had FM, and to my amazement, it sounded far better than an AM signal.

I would lie in front of the speakers on the console stereo, and if a song I liked a lot came on, I'd get up, slide the top across, and turn it up.

Now, radio was personal. The guy talking on the stereo wasn't just on the radio, he was on the radio from down the road.

A few years later, my aunt went to work in a secretarial position at the local station; and I asked, not thinking it possible, if I could go to work with her one day and see how radio worked. Her boss said OK, and I found myself sitting inside a radio station control room with a real, live DJ.

I was hooked. This was what I wanted to do.

During my senior year of high school, one of my classmates dared me to go to the radio station and ask for a job. I took the dare. During lunch, he rode to the station with me, and I walked in and asked for a job. The manager looked at me and said, "Be here Sunday morning at 5:30."

I don't have a recording of my debut, but I'm sure I was awful. Then, he told me to be back next Sunday morning at 5:30. And so it went. That was the beginning of 25 years in the radio business.

I met celebrities, and I met everyday folk just like myself. I was a part of something very special and I knew it. I got paid to have fun. Not many folks can say that.

In the late '90s, I put my journalism degree to use. I do a lot of writing now; but before I left the radio industry, I built a recording studio in my home. It allows me to keep my toe in the water, doing voiceovers for commercials and the like.

Nowadays, radio is mostly run by computers and the DJ has all but gone the way of the blacksmith and the buggy salesman.

But for a quarter century, radio put food on my family's table and fun in my life. It took me from Arkansas to Texas, where I raised a family and completed my broadcasting career.

I still have that Sony AM radio, and it still works. Sometimes, late at night, I tune in voices from far away and smile. And I say a word of thanks to a guy named Steve, who told me to be there Sunday morning at 5:30.

They're Just Like Us, But Famous

Most old-school celebrities are just regular folks.

There are very few celebrities I'll spend money to see, but Jay Leno made the list.

We sat in the audience waiting for him to take the stage, and when he did, he didn't disappoint. He's one of the few comedians who can be nonstop funny for 90 minutes without being vulgar.

We didn't get to meet Jay, but he seems like a nice guy. He has that reputation in the show business community.

As we left the venue to grab a bite to eat, I thought about the celebrities and famous people I've met. In my former career in broadcasting, I met a lot of well-known people. It was part of the job.

Singers were always touring to promote and sell albums, writers were pushing books, actors were plugging their movie or TV series or trying to raise awareness for a charity, and politicians were trying to get re-elected.

As a 17-year-old just starting out, my first few celebrity encounters were nerve-wracking. On live radio, I had to interview Mel Tillis. Fortunately, he was very nice and accommodating. I'm sure he sensed my nervousness and tried to help me out. I'm guessing it's probably the only time in his career when the interviewer stuttered more than he did.

But, the more well-known people I met and interviewed, the more it became obvious that they were just regular people who had worked hard to succeed at what they did. Most of them were very appreciative for what you were doing to help promote their career.

When The Judds first hit the scene, they had one hit under their belt. I interviewed Wynonna backstage at a community college auditorium. She and I were about the same age, and it seemed as if one kid was interviewing another. She was cordial and unassuming.

Just two years later, she and her mom would be one of the biggest acts in country music.

Randy Travis surprised me. He was promoting a new album, and called me from the set of a movie he was filming. I was in the studio doing my show and the interview was live. He stayed on for about half an hour, and then talked to me off-air for another 45 minutes. A genuinely nice guy who was grateful for his success. I feel bad for how things have turned out for his health and pray that he will improve.

I interviewed the beautiful country singer Lorrie Morgan. She made me stutter, too.

Vice President Dan Quayle was the antithesis of how the left in the press portrayed him. He was very articulate and obviously one of the smartest people in the room. I met him when he came to town trying to help him and his boss keep their jobs in the White

House. He looked more like a movie star than a politician. He was striking in looks and talked to you as if you were old friends.

President Bill Clinton was the master of interacting with people. I met him when he was still the governor of Arkansas. I've never seen anyone else work a room full of people like he does. All of his faults aside, he went out of his way to be nice.

Remember Jerry Mathers? Beaver Cleaver from TV? He makes the top five list of nicest celebrities I've worked with. I say worked with, because he spent two days in town on a promotional tour. I was assigned to him to make sure everything went OK, so that included picking him up and taking him where he needed to go. One evening, he addressed a crowd of 800 people and then stayed for photos and autographs of everyone who wanted one. Later, at a restaurant, he greeted everyone who approached him, even though they were interrupting his meal.

I was even able to interview one of my idols. Mel Blanc may not be a name you immediately recognize, but you know his work. He did the voices of more than 1,000 cartoon characters, including Bugs Bunny, Daffy Duck, Yosemite Sam, Sylvester, Tweety and many more for Warner Brothers.

I talked to him by phone in 1984, just five years before he passed. He was so kind and generous. There's nothing quite like hearing Bugs Bunny say your name.

If there's one thing I miss about broadcasting, it's the interaction with the famous people who turn out to be just regular folks.

I didn't get a chance to meet Jay Leno; but Jay, if you're reading this, you rank right up there with Mel in the idol category.

Putting the Band Back Together

Most teenage boys have visions of being a rock star.

Correction: Visions of being a rock star are what they have when they're not having visions of cheerleaders.

As a child of the '70s, my rock-star idols were longhaired, chain-smoking, whiskey-drinking, 20-somethings who made two guitars, a bass and a set of drums sound like a million dollars. At least that's what it sounded like to me. My dad said it sounded like noise.

My parents didn't view these guys the same way that I did.

I mean, how could a bunch of morally bankrupt fellas who had millions of dollars, adoring fans and girls throwing themselves at them while they flew on their own private plane that took them to a mountaintop home that overlooked a valley in California, possibly feel good about themselves?

I was pretty sure I knew the answer.

So, in 1976, my buddies Paul, Doug, Keith and I started our own band. "Freedom" we called it.

It was Paul that came up with the name. It was the bicentennial year.

"Freedom" may seem hokey now, but what else would we have called it? After all, Lynyrd Skynyrd was already taken.

We learned all the basic songs. "Johnny B. Goode," "Proud Mary," "Takin' Care of Business."

And we practiced until we were good enough to play our first, high-profile gig: The Little River County Nursing Home.

The audience was very responsive. I'm pretty sure they couldn't hear us, but they were very responsive.

We also played a street dance. But, mostly we just practiced in my parents' driveway. Mom wouldn't let us play in the house. I think she felt that if she had to suffer, the whole neighborhood should also have to suffer.

Time passed, the band drifted apart and we all went on to different things. I pursued a career in radio and for a while, so did Paul. Doug found a career in paper manufacturing, and honestly, I'm not sure where Keith the drummer is these days.

Paul always kept up his music and today he plays professionally. Doug says he still plays his bass.

Me? I still play guitar every now and then. I also enjoy playing the bass and the banjo.

And those morally bankrupt rock stars on whom I used to heap mounds of adulation? I'm thinking about putting the band back together and heading over to their nursing home to drop off some Dulcolax and play a few choruses of "Takin' Care of Business."

Still Rocking

Kids nowadays may have cooler toys, but my generation had the best bands.

The 1970s produced some of the best music this country has ever seen. The bands that carried myself and other teens through that great decade are still as solid sounding in an mp3 file now as they were from an LP then.

The Beatles broke up in 1970, but the influence they had on their musical descendants lasted at least 10 great years. My love of rock music began with the Beatles, and I still listen to them. But, it was bands such as Led Zeppelin, Boston, The Doobie Brothers, The Eagles, Heart, Foreigner, Journey and Lynyrd Skynyrd that solidified my dedication to what is now called Classic Rock.

In the '70s, a new album by any one of these groups was an event. I can recall the anticipation of the release day. It reminds me of the lines of people I now see on television who wait outside an Apple Store to buy the newest iPhone.

If you want proof that the best bands came from the '70s, just look at who's selling out arenas across the country. I recently tried to buy tickets to see The Eagles and they sold out almost immediately in both Bossier City and Little Rock. Ticket prices started at well over $100, with prices going far beyond that.

Seventies rock music was the glue that bonded American teens. Today, kids have Facebook and Instagram. We had Peter Frampton.

Some of the best times I had were standing next to people I didn't know at all, enjoying a band we all new quite well. The enjoyment was something we shared. It truly was amazing to experience.

I still have virtually all of my old albums, and a working Technics turntable. I love browsing through the albums, pulling one out of the sleeve and cover and placing it on the platter. It is not only nostalgic, vinyl just sounds better than digital.

Putting the needle on cut one of The Eagles "Greatest Hits Volume One," listening through side one, flipping it over and continuing through side two takes me back to different times, people and places.

I don't know what it is about music, but unlike most other experiences in our lives, songs are forever tied to memories both good and bad. A specific tune can remind me of someone who's no longer here, or the cheeseburger basket at Herb's I was enjoying the first time I heard it.

The rock music of the '70s has held up. There are local and satellite radio stations dedicated to it. Very few other eras of music can say that.

A reunion of a classic rock band is an event. When Led Zeppelin reunited in 2006 for a one-off tribute concert, millions of people almost crashed the website trying to buy tickets.

Thirty years from now, I highly doubt anyone will say "Do you think the Spice Girls will ever get back together?"

Young people today may have more and cooler electronics, but they also have Justin Bieber.

My generation will always have the best bands.

The only problem I have with Classic Rock is that they aren't making it anymore.

Go, Johnny, Go

I had no idea how much one musician had impacted my life until Chuck Berry died.

When I was 8 years old, I knew that I wanted to play Rock and Roll music. What I didn't know was that Chuck almost singlehandedly gave Rock and Roll the roots of its sound and paved the road to success for all rock acts who would follow, including The Beatles and The Rolling Stones.

I remember walking into Mike Hubrel's bedroom in 1970 to sit down for my first guitar lesson. It was a stark contrast. Mike's hair was long, and his walls were covered with cool posters and photos of rock stars of the day.

My hair was short, and I didn't have cool posters or photos of rock stars of the day. My father would never have approved of either.

About 10 years older than me, Mike had a modern, electric guitar that glistened and looked expensive. I had my dad's acoustic, which was almost as big as I was and likely cost a few dollars at Sears and Roebuck when Eisenhower was president.

Mike asked me what I wanted to learn. My answer was Rock and Roll.

Now, some guitar teachers would have insisted that you first learn music theory, scales, and how to read music. Not Mike. He taught me the chords A, D, and E.

I had no idea at the time, but he had given me the keys to Rock and Roll.

On those three chords, Chuck Berry built "Johnny B. Goode," "Maybelline," "No Particular Place To Go," "Roll Over, Beethoven," and dozens of other songs that would become the foundation of a genre of music that would give pleasure to multiple generations for decades to come.

Chuck blended country music with rhythm and blues. He wasn't the first to do this, but what Chuck did that others hadn't done was write smart lyrics that every person – rich or poor, black or white – could relate to. He wrote about cars, school, girls, money, and he showed that he was a learned individual.

In "Roll Over, Beethoven," he wrote:

You know, my temperature's risin'
And the jukebox blows a fuse
My heart's beatin' rhythm
And my soul keeps on singin' the blues
Roll over, Beethoven, and tell Tchaikovsky the news

I wasn't around in the mid-'50s, but I'm guessing that Mr. Berry introduced many a young radio listener to the names Beethoven and Tchaikovsky.

In an interview I watched on YouTube, Chuck explained that, as a young man, he was very much into poetry. Unlike many of his generation, he not only finished high school, but had some education beyond that.

He grew up in a middle-class neighborhood. His father was a contractor and a deacon in the church, and his mother was a high school principal. Chuck got work playing his music in clubs. His father would never have approved of either, the music or the clubs.

So, in the early days, he appeared on marquees as Chuck Berryne.

By age 14, I was in my first band, my hair was long, and the walls of my room were covered with cool posters and photos of rock stars of the day. My dad still didn't approve.

Much to the chagrin of the neighbors, the band often practiced at my house. One of the first songs we learned was "Johnny B. Goode." That one song broke the ice between me and my dad.

One day when we were playing it, I looked up to see my father standing in the doorway smiling and tapping his foot. He may not have approved of the hair or the posters, but he approved of Chuck Berry.

I would go on to join other bands, and whether I was in a rock band or a country band, "Johnny B. Goode" was always on our set list. From the stage, you could see everyone leaving their chairs and heading to the dance floor when the opening riff began. They would smile and sing as they danced.

I have to say, there's no better feeling than playing "Johnny B. Goode" in front of an audience.

The Beatles and Stones would surpass and outsell Chuck Berry, but they all revered him. John Lennon recounted the first time he met him with a look of unworthiness and awe. Keith Richards of The Rolling Stones threw a 60th birthday party for Chuck in 1987, and he and Eric Clapton were part of Chuck's backup band.

Chuck Berry accomplished more in his life than he got credit for. He broke down racial barriers with his music. Some of his biggest fans in the early years were white kids. Chuck opened one of the first night clubs that wasn't segregated. And he wrote timeless songs that were the building blocks for a type of music that now has its own hall of fame in Cleveland.

When the Rock and Roll Hall of Fame opened in the 1980s, Chuck was one of the first inductees. Rightfully so.

Chuck passed away at his St. Louis-area home at age 90. He had recently recorded a new album. It will be released this year.

He gave us more than we gave him.

Thanks, Chuck, for everything.

CHAPTER SEVEN – RELIVING THE PAST

In the Game Show Realm, 'Match Game' is Unmatched

Once upon a time, daytime television was filled with game shows, people winning prizes, and funny celebrities. I miss those days, and one game show in particular: "Match Game."

During the midday hours of our summer breaks in the mid-1970s, just about the only thing on TV that a kid wanted to watch were game shows.

We stayed with my grandmother during those summer days. She watched game shows too, but she mainly watched soap operas, or as she called them, her "stories." You could cheer and talk during game shows, but not during her stories. Talking during "Days Of Our Lives" or "As The World Turns" would get you sent outside to play.

There were dozens of game shows on during this era. "Jeopardy," "Let's Make A Deal," "The $10,000 Pyramid," "The Newlywed Game," "Hollywood Squares," "Password," and "The Price Is Right" (I attended a live taping of "The Price Is Right" in the '80s, but that's another story) were just a few of the best examples.

In my shop, I currently have a TV with an antenna. I can pick up all of the local channels, many of which aren't carried on cable or satellite. Whenever I'm working on a project, I like to turn the set on and tune it to sports or an old cop show, such as "Columbo." The background noise keeps me company.

During a recent project, I found myself stopping my project and turning to watch the TV. What caught my ear was the distinctive theme music of "Match Game," and the show's announcer, Johnny Olson. Johnny was introducing Brett Somers, Richard Dawson, Charles Nelson Reilly and others.

Soon after, I was sitting in a chair and playing the game along with a gentleman who was wearing a pretty awful leisure suit and with a lady whose hair was a copy of Dorothy Hamill's.

My broken lawn mower would have to wait.

"Match Game" was hosted by a man I consider to have been the best game show host of the era, Gene Rayburn. Gene had the rare ability to herd cats. In this case, herd celebrity cats.

The show consisted of six celebrity panelists who tried to match their answer to a contestant's answer, through a humorous and almost always risqué-sounding question.

Gene would ask the fill-in-the-blank question, and the six celebrities would each write down their own answer on a card. They would then place the card into a slot in front of them. When all slots were filled, the celebrities' names would light up, indicating that they were done.

Gene would then turn to whichever contestant's turn it was and ask them for their answer. Each celebrity would then reveal what they had written down.

The more matches a contestant had, the more money they won.

But, as I mentioned, risqué answers were what the show's writers were going for. The trick was for each celebrity to answer the double entendre question with a response that matched the contestant's.

"Dumb Dora was either pouring gravy on George's (blank)," or "Dumb Donald was using Suzie's (blank) as an ashtray."

You get the idea.

But, the "Match Game" that became a hit and spawned three additional incarnations of itself, was almost canceled before it got started.

In 1962, game show kingpin Mark Goodson thought he had a flop on his hands. Gene Rayburn was the host, but the ratings were terrible. Questions such as, "Name the color of a flower," and "What's America's favorite holiday?" weren't cutting it. The show was boring, and the network canceled it.

The show's writer, a man named Dick DeBartolo, who was also a writer at Mad Magazine, called Goodson and asked for a meeting. On his website, DeBartolo said that he asked for more of a Mad approach to writing the questions. He said that Goodman told him that NBC couldn't cancel the show twice, so with the six weeks the show had left, he could write what he wanted.

The ratings climbed, then soared, and for the next two decades, Gene Rayburn herded celebrity cats with great success.

In 1976, Richard Dawson left to host "Family Feud," which, ironically, would overtake "Match Game" in the ratings and lead to the latter's demise.

"Match Game" was canceled in 1982.

But, through cable channels, including the Game Show Network, "Match Game" has been rediscovered by its original fans and by new fans, such as college students.

Three other attempts, with varying levels of success, have resurrected "Match Game" using different hosts. The latest is on ABC with actor Alec Baldwin.

However, none of the newer versions will ever recreate the magic of Gene Rayburn, Brett Somers, Richard Dawson and Charles Nelson Reilly.

If one does and proves me wrong, I'll be happy to go down to my shop and pull the plug on my (blank).

Just My Type

For those who know me, it's no secret that I enjoy perusing the classifieds for yard or estate sales. But, a recent online visit to the local Craigslist site led to the purchase of a manual typewriter. A 1958 Remington Quiet-Riter, to be exact.

This story was written on it.

Some might consider an almost-60-year-old typewriter a nonsensical purchase, considering that desktops, laptops and iPads (the latter typically being my chosen device for writing) are much easier to navigate and correct mistakes.

All of these assertions regarding modern technology are true, but there's just something special about a typewriter. And I decided that I wanted one.

I called the number in the Craigslist ad and an older gentleman answered. I rattled off the typical questions I normally ask regarding anything I'm interested in buying, especially if it's an older item. Does it still work? Any problems with it? What kind of shape is it in? And, most importantly, why are you selling it?

He explained that when he was in high school in the late 1950s, his grandmother offered to buy him a typewriter if he would take a typing class. He agreed, she bought the typewriter and he took the class; but he said that he had to be honest that he never learned to type very well.

In the '50s, taking typing was not considered very manly. I can only imagine how unmanly it was since I took typing 20 years later in the late 1970s.

In 1977, my buddy Steve and I needed to choose an elective in school. We selected typing class. We picked typing, not because we thought we'd ever really use it much, but because we were 15 and the class was filled with girls.

Once we were in the class, Steve and I quickly realized that typing was no blow-off course. Typing was difficult. It was especially difficult for two guys in a sea of girls. Mrs. Lewis gave all of the new IBM electric typewriters to them, and Steve and I were relegated to the leftover World War II era Underwood manual models.

Once it became obvious that the girls weren't going to notice us any more in a typing class than they did in study hall, we decided to make typing a competition.

Anyone who's ever taken typing knows that speed and accuracy are how you're graded. Each day, we would try to outdo the other. Bragging rights became just as important as making a good grade.

I can recall the day that I typed 27 words per minute with no errors. That doesn't sound like much, but I'm telling you, try it today on a manual typewriter and you'll see it's not easy.

Steve and I continued our typing competition and by year's end, both of us were very proficient.

I would later determine that typing was the most valuable class I've ever taken.

Scarcely a year after typing class, I was accepted into the journalism class, to work on the student newspaper and high school annual. The year after that, I was hired at the local radio station, which required the ability to rapidly gather, type and report the news.

The man with the Craigslist ad agreed to meet me in a local grocery store parking lot during my lunch hour. He pulled the typewriter case out of his shiny new truck and placed it on the tailgate. It was quite a contrast; the old typewriter sitting on the back of a modern pickup.

He opened the case and I was very surprised. When he told me that he never really learned to type, I could see why. The Remington looked virtually unused. It was like opening a time capsule.

The original manual was still in the bottom of the case. A woman with a '50s hairdo and wearing clothing from the period smiled at me from the cover as she happily typed.

The keys still had the newness to them. None of the letters or symbols were faded.

We agreed on a price. I paid him, took the typewriter back to work, and later home.

I surprised myself with how much I remembered regarding the operation of a manual typewriter. How to feed a sheet of paper, where the lever was to move the carriage back and forth ... it all came back to me.

What I had forgotten was how many of the symbols have been moved. The apostrophe on a typewriter is used by holding down the shift key and punching the number 8. The quotation mark is found by holding the shift key and punching the number 2.

On today's computers, those two symbols are typically found to the right of the colon and semicolon key. On typewriters, the key to the right of the colon and semicolon key includes the @ and ¢ symbols.

The underline key on a modern keyboard is found above the letter P. On a typewriter, you hold the shift key and punch the number 6. Typewriters also have a key for ½ and ¼. Try finding those on a new keyboard.

I have no idea why these symbols were moved from their original locations, but I had to relearn where they were originally to write this column.

One of the most interesting things I learned about typewriters is that, when adjusted for inflation, they used to cost more than many of today's computers.

On YouTube, I found a TV commercial from 1958 selling my typewriter. It features two girls chatting on the phone. One of them is beaming with glee because her Remington Quiet-Riter was the inspiration for a play she had written, which was about to be staged by the local drama club.

Suddenly, a pitchman appears in the ad, explaining how affordable the new typewriters are. The Remington ranges from $84 to $133. "Get yours for only $5 down and $1.50 per week, plus carrying charges," he says.

Carrying charges is a 1950s term for interest.

I went online and found an inflation converter. If you bought this typewriter in 1958 for $133, that's the equivalent of $1,110.72 in today's money.

Reversing the same calculator, I entered in the $35 I paid the gentleman for his typewriter and discovered that I got a great deal. I paid $4.19 in 1958 money.

I'm appreciative for the great deal he made me, and I'm guessing that his grandmother might have been appreciative that the Remington went to someone who is finally using it.

The truth is, I'm a low-tech kinda guy. My percolator is older than I am, I like old cars better than new ones, and writing this on a typewriter brought me joy and a lot of memories.

It also filled the house with a sound that reminded me of a time when Steve and I tried, but failed, to get the girls' attention.

The Dream Car

It was the car I'd always wanted. A 1971 Oldsmobile Cutlass 442 Convertible.

I found it one morning while cruising (pun intended) on eBay. The guy who owned it and had it for sale lived just east of me, a few miles across the Louisiana state line.

It was red, with large white stripes on the hood. From the photos, it looked to be in great condition for a 32-year-old car. I stared at it on the computer screen.

I wanted this car.

My love of classic cars dates back to my first years of driving in the mid-'70s. Like most kids at that time, my first car would be an older one. Only rich kids got new cars. I knew very few rich kids, and I certainly wasn't one of them.

I consider those who are my age to be among the most fortunate when it comes to first automobiles. Cars like our late-'60s and early-'70s Chevys, Oldsmobiles, Fords and Pontiacs, are now selling for lots of dough at car auctions, such as Barrett-

Jackson. And they were downright cool and fun to drive.

My very first car was a 1966 Ford Mustang that my dad picked up for $500. You couldn't buy a set of hubcaps for that car now for $500.

But, it would be my next car that would cause me to, some 30 years later, stare at a picture on the Internet at that 442 for sale in Louisiana.

My dad paid for my first vehicle, but in 1978, I bought my first car. It was a 1972 Oldsmobile Cutlass Supreme. Metallic gold, it had a 350 V8, bucket seats, and a console with an automatic transmission. I paid $1,000 for it, and some of the best memories of my life came from that car.

But, any Oldsmobile Cutlass lover at that time always had an eye for the 442. The 442 was the sport version of the Olds Cutlass.

Many people erroneously think that 442 is the size of the engine. But, 442 stands for 4-speed, 4-barrel (carburetor), and dual exhaust. The engine options were a 350-cubic-inch, or the 455.

After leaving home to raise my own family, I would own a variety of classic cars. Among them were another 1966 Mustang, a 1971 Cutlass Sport Coupe, a 1972 Chevy pickup, and others. But, I never really got the 442 out of my head.

And there it was. Staring back at me.

116

My wife and I discussed it and, being the good sport that she is, she agreed to let me buy the car.

I contacted the guy and made him an offer to end the auction early. He accepted it, and a buddy of mine agreed to drive me to Louisiana to pick it up.

When we arrived, it looked even better in person than it did in the photos.

I asked him why he was willing to part with it, and he gave me an answer you hear often from classic car lovers. He had another car project he needed the money for.

I drove the car home, smiling the whole way. For the next five years, the 442 was part of the family. It would be featured in of one of our children's wedding, it took me back to my hometown for visits, and it was in a number of car shows.

But, like anything worth having, classic cars take time.

One evening, I was standing in the garage looking at the 442. It occurred to me that I couldn't remember the last time I'd driven it. If you can't remember the last time you've driven a car you own, it's probably a sign that you don't really need it.

This wasn't long after we'd moved to the country. I needed a tractor, and here sat a car that really should belong to someone who had more time to give it.

I put the car on eBay. A man in Galveston won the auction.

When he and his wife arrived at our home to pick it up, he had the same smile on his face that I did when I bought it. The car was going to a good home. That was all I needed to see to be able to let it go.

As he got ready to drive it away, I told him to wait a moment. I went into the house and grabbed a 442 ball cap that I had. I went back outside and placed it on his head. I told him to hold on to it, because convertibles tend to make you lose your hat.

He went back to Galveston, and I went to the tractor dealership.

I thought about that 442 convertible this weekend as I used my tractor to move a dead pine tree from our pasture. I still miss that car a little, but the tractor is far more practical.

And, I can say something that most guys my age can't. I once owned the car of my dreams.

CHAPTER EIGHT – SPECIAL FOLKS

True Friendships Never Fade

There are only a few real friends we have in life. We may have hundreds or even thousands of acquaintances, but real friends, we only have a few.

While fulfilling my civic obligation at jury duty, my phone vibrated. I was sitting there watching people give the judge their excuses on why they should be allowed to go home, so I welcomed the interruption.

I looked down and saw that it was a text from a high school buddy. In the last few years he and I have stayed in touch mostly by texting, sometimes by phone, rarely face-to-face. But decades ago in high school, we were inseparable.

9:21 a.m. – (text of funny cartoon)

9:22 a.m. – "Awesome. Jury duty today. Hope you're well," I replied.

No response.

I put my phone back in its holster and thought about all we'd done together, good and bad, and what a great friend he is. I looked around the room at the jury pool and wondered how many truly great friends each of them might have.

Not many, was my guess.

Shortly thereafter, something that never happens at jury duty happened. All cases were settled and every potential juror was released. What started out as a morning I had dreaded was turning out much better than expected.

With my $6 in hand, I made my way back to my car, got in, and drove into the rest of my day.

3:56 p.m. – "Want to drink a cup of coffee with me?"

3:56 p.m. – "Where are you?" I responded.

3:57 p.m. – "IHOP"

My buddy doesn't even live in Texas, yet he'd been texting me all day from my own area, where he had patiently waited to contact me a second time when he thought I might be out of jury duty.

3:57 p.m. – "On my way."

His job requires him to travel all over the U.S., and he'd had a layover about 45 minutes away, so he contacted me. I was pleased that he did. The last time we'd visited in person was about five years ago.

We went through two hours and a lot of caffeine fairly quickly. We talked about our adventures, our successes, our failures and our futures. We discussed our families and our careers, and the paths that led to them. We laughed at times. We were serious at times.

120

And just as suddenly as our impromptu gathering had come together, it ended.

I had to get back home, and so did he. He was anxious to see his wife and I wanted to go home and see mine.

We tipped the waiter and went back to our lives.

6:45 p.m.

As I drove home, I thought about what makes a good friendship and how one lasts for four decades.

It's pretty simple, really. It's the ability to just pick up the last conversation you had five years ago, right where it left off.

And Sew it Goes

My friend's mother had passed away and my friend had the unenviable task of sorting through her mom's things. She had decided what she was going to keep, but now she had to price the remaining items, advertise the sale, and then watch as strangers came through her mom's home and took them away.

I've gone to estate sales, yard sales and garage sales (there are many names for them) all of my life. Some of the best things I've come across and either found a good home for or kept and used, came from sales such as these.

121

But this particular sale was different. It was going to change people's lives.

My friend's mom was a quilter. She lived a modest life, from what I could tell from her home. I was invited to come ahead of the sale, so I was able to roam freely, my friend by my side, and not have to dodge dozens of other people trying to find a deal for themselves.

The tour of the house was guided. My friend explained what we were seeing. This item her mom had acquired when she was a young woman. That item was bought when my friend and her brother were little. Each thing had a memory attached to it, no matter how common or unique each were.

I bought a hand-crank coffee grinder and one or two other things, but the area I kept coming back to was the room filled with all of the quilting items.

Everything was compartmentalized. The needles and thread had their place, as did the measuring tapes and strips, and the cutters that were used to precisely make quilt squares.

But what I was amazed by was the sheer volume of fabric. There were baskets full of fabric everywhere I looked. Some of it had already been cut and sewn into partial quilt tops, while others were in squares, while others were still large bolts of fabric that had been neatly folded and left for the day that she intended to come back to it for a specific project.

There was a lot of Christmas fabric. A whole lot.

I asked my friend what her mom did with all of her quilts. She said that she gave them away.

She talked about how her mother had made quilts for those in hospice, others who were in need, those she just liked and wanted them to have a quilt, and the many that she made for veterans and children.

If you or anyone close to you has ever quilted, you know how many hours, weeks, and sometimes months it can take to complete a project, based on its complexity.

Quilting used to be part of what most women in a Southern family learned. It was out of necessity. I can remember going to visit my father's parents, and almost always, my dad's mom had a quilt frame set up in the living room and was working on a quilt for someone.

I never paid too much attention to it then, but now I wish that I had. I'd give anything to go back in time and ask my grandmother how she learned to sew and quilt, who the quilts were for, and why she liked making them.

Since my wife quilts, I looked around the room of my friend's mom's home that was filled with all of the quilting materials and had a thought.

"How much for all of the fabric?" I asked. "All?" she replied. "Yes, everything," I said.

123

She asked me if I was sure that I wanted to take all of it. After all, I hadn't looked through it with any deep digging, and I'm sure that she knew that me being a guy, I knew virtually less than nothing about what I was asking to purchase.

She was correct, but I had a feeling that I should buy it all.

We made a deal. I loaded it all up in my car and brought it home.

My wife was both stunned and intrigued. For a moment, I wasn't sure whether I was going to get a kiss or a tongue-lashing. After she got over the basket after basket that I had brought in from the car and stacked in her sewing room, I sensed that I probably wasn't going to get a kiss or a tongue-lashing. I'd have to let some time go by to find out whether I'd made the right decision.

It took a long time for her to wash and press all of the different pieces of fabric, sort through the Christmas pieces, both blocks and partially finished sections, and arrange all of it in a way that it seemed organized to her.

The local Methodist church had a quilting group. My wife heard about it. She attended a couple of their meetings to see if she liked it.

She did. She loved it.

She would come home from the gatherings and talk about a quilt that one of the members had made for hospice, or another who was making one for someone they knew. My wife went into detail about someone that a member of the group knew who everyone felt could use a quilt. And she talked about the quilts they made for the children.

Slowly, many of the baskets I brought home from my friend's mom's estate now contain less and less fabric.

And lots of deserving people continue to receive a quilt of their own, thanks to two ladies who never met, but shared two things: a selfless love for others, and a God-given talent for making quilts.

CHAPTER NINE – THEY HAVE FOUR LEGS AND THEY'RE FAMILY

Bert the Dog

He came to us when he was between 5 and 7 years old.

We'll never know exactly how old he is because the people who drove to the dead-end road in front of our home, removed his collar, dumped him out, and drove away, didn't leave a note.

It was a 102-degree July day in 2006.

He came to the sliding glass door on the back of our house and stood there waiting to be let in. I would assume it was exactly what he did at their home before they decided that he wasn't worth keeping.

"Whose dog is that?" I asked my wife.

"Maybe it's the neighbors'," she said. "They take in lots of rescues."

I called the neighbor, but after describing the small terrier mix with big eyes, "No," the neighbor said. It wasn't theirs.

After heading outside to see about him, I could see where he'd had a collar and it was no longer there. He was hot. I gave him cold water.

I checked with the other neighbors. Nope. No one's dog. But one neighbor informed me that dog-dumping was common on our street.

We had lived in our country neighborhood for only a couple of years. I liked everything about the neighborhood until I was told that.

Our previous dog had just died of heart disease and, emotionally, neither of us was in much of a mindset to take on another dog.

"He can stay outside on the porch and if he's still here in a week, we'll think about keeping him," my wife said as he jumped up in her lap.

He was such a loveable guy, I kept thinking that maybe whoever dumped him would realize their mistake and return for him.

I made him a place to sleep outside in the shade under the fan and put out food and water.

And each day, like an 8-year-old boy, I'd awake to see if he was still there. Afternoons, I would come home and ask if he was still there. "Check out back," she would say. He always was.

We gave him lots of attention. He liked it there. I was glad.

One Friday, I came home and he wasn't out back. "Where is he?" I asked. She pointed to the couch.

There was a lump under the blanket. He was obviously a burrower, and he was obviously staying.

"He has bug eyes like a scientist. Let's name him Egbert," I said. "No, we're not naming him Egbert," she responded. "But we can name him Bert."

And so we did.

Bert has been with us through many family changes. The loss of family members, the births of new ones, anniversaries, birthdays, good times and tough times. He's been our friend.

Of late, I had lost sight of what he has meant to us. His gradual instability, accidents and increased medical care have frustrated me.

My friend, who used to be agile and attentive, now is frequently underfoot or sleeping a lot.

My attitude was bad, and I came to realize it. I believe that most, if not all, of my frustration is the inability to accept that this relationship is nearing the end.

Life is a cycle. There is a beginning and an end. We struggle at the beginning, and we struggle at the end.

I don't know how much longer Bert will be with us, but that 8-year-old boy inside of me is sure glad that of all of the houses in our neighborhood he could have chosen nine years ago, he picked ours.

Cats are Smarter Than Dogs

You can name a cat whatever you'd like, but they all think their name is "Here, Kitty, Kitty, Kitty."

Cat owners and dog owners are equally passionate about their chosen pet; but since I own one of each, I feel qualified to make the observation that cats are smarter than dogs.

Oh, sure, you can train a dog to answer to their given name, catch a Frisbee, fetch a paper, slippers and other such things; but cats have managed to train people.

Think about it. A cat is the only pet that can convince a human to repeatedly get out of their chair and let them back in the house two minutes after they were just let out. This can occur three or four times and the human responds each time without complaining. I suspect that cats do this for their own amusement.

The bottom line is that people own dogs, but cats own people.

Our cat, Spooky, came with the house.

When we purchased our home in summer 2003, I arrived with the first load of boxes and began to stack them in the garage. Suddenly, a beautiful, but mouthy, black cat appeared and began winding between my feet as I tried to work. She talked to me loudly, but I didn't understand what she wanted. I finally realized that this cat was hungry.

It was after-hours, so I drove to the nearest convenience store and bought an overpriced box of Little Friskies. I returned home, poured some food into a makeshift container made from a small cardboard box, and the cat finally quieted down. "Good," I thought. "Now, this cat will go home."

Nope.

She hung around for a week or so and then one day, a blonde girl who appeared to be about 12 rang the doorbell. "Have you seen my cat, Spooky?" she asked. She explained that she was one of the previous residents and that she thought maybe her cat had come back here.

By now, we had become attached to the cat; so letting go of her wasn't easy. But, we returned her cat to her and she left, one happy little girl.

Two days later as I was unpacking boxes in the garage, I hear a familiar mewing behind me. There was Spooky. This was her house and she was determined to live here. Once again, the little girl returned later that day, retrieved her cat and left.

The next day, the cat came back. But, the little girl never did.

Spooky had told all of the humans what she was going to do, and that was that.

In 2006, a dog we didn't recognize showed up out of nowhere at our back door on a hot, July day. We welcomed him into our home. You could see where he'd had a collar, it had been removed, and he'd obviously been abandoned near our home. No problem, he would now live with us. He needed a place to stay.

Spooky didn't like the new company and she disappeared for three days. But, eventually, she came home and slowly warmed up to Bert the Dog. They're now best buddies.

Spooky is now showing signs of age. She's not as quick as she used to be at catching the mice, moles and other things cats do to earn their keep. She has to eat a special food, and she sleeps a lot more than she used to.

Cats call the shots in their lives, and humans could learn a lot from them. Like cats, we should listen more to ourselves than to what others tell us we should do and how we should do it.

However, I don't want to sound as if I think cats are completely selfish. That's not true at all.

After all, Spooky has allowed us to live in her house for 11 years now.

And she still thinks her name is "Here, Kitty, Kitty, Kitty."

CHAPTER TEN – LIFE ON THE HOMESTEAD

Country Living

Walking down the sloped driveway, newspaper in hand, I strain to see the house, which is shrouded in fog.

As I pass the truck parked in the drive, the mist has frosted the glass and offers the illusion of being covered in ice.

The quiet is broken by a single crow announcing his presence as he pierces the fog near the chimney. He veers to my left, on the way to the rest of his day. The cat greets me near the front door and escorts me inside.

It is a typical Saturday in the country. I sip my Folgers, which was poured from the spout of a 1960 Universal Coffeematic percolator, and begin to read my paper.

Nature begins to stir, and her sounds make their way through the screen door on the back patio and through an open window in the front of the house. It has a stereo-like effect, and it is comforting.

Completing the newspaper crossword puzzles, I rise from my chair and put on my shop clothes.

Long ago, my wife tactfully implemented a rule about which clothes can be worn in the shop. No nice shirts or pants are allowed, not even if my intention is to only a make a quick trip and come back. It seems that I'm easily distracted and somehow will start a project while I'm there, which can cause nice clothes to become shop clothes.

The birds speak to me as I make the short trek down the hill from the house to the shop. They tell me of their happiness to be here. A mockingbird flits from an oak to a pine and back again.

I insert the key in the shop's padlock, and the loud click breaks nature's monopoly of the morning sounds.

I flip on the shop light, turn on the classic country station, and sip my percolator coffee as I begin to assess the projects that made my mental list during the week. The steering replacement parts for one of the lawnmowers have arrived, but I decide to table that project in favor of savoring a few more minutes of what's left of the morning.

The sun begins to burn off the fog. As the veil slowly begins to lift, the beauty that surrounds me emerges. The windmill in the neighbor's pasture slowly turns with the light breeze. The dew glistens on the top of the coastal grass in our pasture. Soon, the coastal will be cut, bailed and rolled, and will become winter meals for someone's cattle and horses.

I finish my coffee and climb into my truck. I decide that a haircut is in order. As I arrive at my barber's shop, which is located on the lake, I see fishermen unloading their boats and preparing for the day's catch. I smile and go inside.

My barber has been my friend for almost 40 years. As she trims my graying hair, she talks about her grandchildren and I talk about mine.

I head back home and back down to the shop. As I pull my truck in front of the open doors, my neighbor arrives on his ATV and discusses his list of projects for the day. We agree to help each other, just as we have most weekends for the past 13 years.

Before the day is over, I will weld, grind on metal, paint, do an oil change, and drink a few beers with my neighbor.

For some, all of this would seem monotonous, boring, or too much like work. For me, it is a gift.

Growing up in a small town in Arkansas, it felt like living in the country, but it was city living. If you can buy a loaf of bread or a gallon of milk within two minutes of leaving your house, you're living in the city.
 After a week of long hours, meetings and deadlines, a whole lot of not much is just what I need.

And every Saturday like this one is a gift from the good Lord above.

Garden of Eatin'

At first, it looked like an onion sitting on the counter. As I got closer, the end still looked just looked like an onion, but it was actually the first yellow squash from our spring garden.

The onions won't be far behind.

There is a sense of independence and pride that comes with being able to walk out your back door and harvest most, if not all, of your evening meal.

I can't take much credit for our garden, because my wife does virtually all of the work.

However, I do enjoy cooking and I love having the ability to go outside with an empty bowl and return with it full of jalapeño peppers, tomatoes, peas, and other homegrown vegetables that can be made into a meal.

Gardening is enjoying a resurgence. I believe that part of it is the fulfilling aspect of gardening as a hobby, but I also think that like my wife and I, many folks want to know exactly what they're eating.

Genetically modified anything isn't appealing to me, especially not when it relates to the fuel that we put into our bodies.

Growing up in Southwest Arkansas, virtually everyone I knew, my family included, had a garden. It was not my favorite thing, for sure. The itchiness of the okra and tomatoes and the sweat pouring down in my eyes from the hot summer are still fresh in my mind. So are the memories of sharing that bounty with family members who are no longer with us.

Families then were known for their skills at raising certain types of vegetables or fruit. One man was famous for the size of his watermelons. Another was renowned for the size and sweetness of his corn. One lady could grow bigger tomatoes than most others.

People would trade what they were good at growing with others who were good at growing something else.

It wasn't uncommon for me to be sitting in the living room on Beech Street watching "Sanford and Son" or another of my favorite shows, when I'd hear someone call through the screen door.

"Yoo hoo! Anybody home?" they'd say.

It might be a neighbor or a relative. They'd come calling with their bags of bounty.

"Yes, sir," or "Yes, ma'am," I'd respond.

They'd let themselves in when they heard me answer, then ask where my mother was. I'd ask them to have a seat and then I'd track down my mom, who might be hanging clothes out to dry on the line, or might actually be in the garden.

My mom would come in the house and be surprised and smile. She would thank them for coming by and then offer them some of what she had grown and harvested.

Dropping off some of your garden's produce was a means to an end. It not only allowed you to show off what you knew how to raise, it was also a reason to visit and drink coffee. It was face time with people you cared for.

Most of those folks are gone now.

Today, my wife raises lettuce, cabbage, tomatoes, peppers, peas, onions, garlic, herbs, and of course squash.

My job is to keep an eye out for the rabbits and run them out of the garden when I see them. Unfortunately, I seem to be failing miserably. The evidence of their frequent visits is undeniable.

But, visits from friends and relatives are also taking place. Yesterday, one of our kids left with the squash I thought looked like an onion, and a bag of peas. My wife will likely repeat her barter transactions of years past and trade some of her produce for others' vegetables, or honey from some friends we know who raise bees.

It's truly amazing what a small patch of God's green earth can give us. It's more than vegetables. Its face time with people who won't always be here.

137

CHAPTER ELEVEN – LOVE AND MARRIAGE

There Should Be a Marriage Manual

When a man asks a woman to marry him, the woman gets a wedding shower. The man gets a bachelor party.

Women are practical. They give the bride-to-be kitchen towels, a Crockpot, frying pan, bedding, dishes, cookware, an iron and silverware.

The groom's buddies give him a hangover.

What they should give the guy is an instruction booklet.

The marriage instruction booklet should be written by really old men who have been married at least 50 years.

If you are a guy, what they never tell you about marriage before you take the leap is that knowing how to communicate with your wife gives you a decided advantage over other men who do not.

Most newlyweds experience miscommunication within 12 minutes of saying, "I do."

Her: "Well, if you don't know, I'm not going to tell you."

Him: (Hangs head and wishes he had an instruction booklet)

There are certain pieces of information regarding how women communicate, which would be very helpful to a young, newly married fella.

One of the most important is that most women don't come right out and tell you some things. They expect you to pay attention and notice them yourself.

Hair is a big one.

Many women are willing to spend more money on a hairdo than most guys would spend on a Holley 780 double-pumper carburetor for their classic car. And that's saying a lot.

Woe to the husband who walks through the door at the end of the day and doesn't catch that his wife got her hair done.

However, this same expectation of noticing things without being told can be a trick. A wife will get a new dress and expect you to notice. She will then wait three years to wear it again to see if you remember.

Him: "Hey, I love the new dress."

Her: "It's three years old."
Him: (Grits teeth)

The marriage instruction booklet should also have a chapter on proper gift-giving.

A Zebco 33 rod and reel, a bowling ball, or a Remington 1100 gas-operated, semi-automatic shotgun might seem like great anniversary gifts for your wife; but trust me, they are not. This was a lesson I learned at a young age. I won't say who the man was who tried this, but my dad can tell you.

Another chapter the marriage instruction booklet should contain is a detailed section on nodding.

When a woman begins to tell you about another woman's love life, just nod. It sounds easy, but putting nodding into play as a practical application can be difficult. Men have a tendency to make comments during these types of conversations, but that is a bad idea.

Incorrect:

Her: "So, she said that he wasn't sure if he was ready to commit right now. They've been dating for a year now, and can you believe that he gave her a rod and reel for her birthday?"

Him: "Was it a Zebco 33?"

Correct:

"So, she said that he wasn't sure if he was ready to commit right now. They've been dating for a year

140

now, and can you believe that he gave her a rod and reel for her birthday?"

Him: (Nods)

The marriage instruction booklet should close with a chapter on when to notice that she wants something. Many women will drop subtle hints about an item that has caught her eye and she would like to have.

But again, a man has to notice the message that is being sent.

Incorrect:

Her: "While I was playing bridge at Nelda's, I noticed that she has a beautiful new throw rug that she found at Bed Bath and Beyond."

Him: "Is that next to the place that sells Zebco 33's?"

Correct:

Just nod.

And go buy her the rug.

Marriage is a Funny Thing

Married folks always have great stories, and some stories are more amusing to one spouse than the other.

Over a Christmas holiday, we went home to Arkansas to visit family. Christmas seems to be the time when everyone whips out their favorite story on another family member, but the stories spouses tell on each other normally are the best.

My mom's friend is like many women when it comes to automobiles. She knows how to operate one, but isn't too keen on any details regarding how they work or much else.

Years ago, mom's friend pulled into a store where she saw her husband's truck parked. He was supposed to have taken her car that day for maintenance, and she was not happy when she spotted his vehicle.

She was late for work and not in the mood to have a conversation with him about his lack of thoughtfulness regarding her and her vehicle's immediate needs. So, she parked her car and got into his truck.

Disgusted by how full his ashtrays were, she pulled them out and emptied them in the nearest trashcan. She then got back in the truck and tidied the rest of the cab up a bit.

Not only had he forgotten about her car, his truck was a mess.

He had left the keys in the ignition (not an uncommon practice in those days), so she cranked up the truck, revved the engine a few times, and drove on to her job.

After a bit, one of her coworkers asked where her car was and whose truck she was driving. She told her the story of how her husband had failed miserably at remembering her vehicle maintenance, but that she had him back on track now after switching vehicles.

Her coworker said, "That's not your husband's truck."

"Yes, it is," she responded.

"No, it's not. Your husband's truck is blue. That truck is red."

Silence.

"You'd better call the police," her coworker said. "I'm sure that truck has been reported stolen."

"I ain't calling anybody," she said. "I'll be right back."

She returned the truck to the spot where it had been parked, got into her vehicle and returned to work.

143

She swore her coworker to secrecy.

A few months later while sitting in the stands at a football game, she overheard a man behind her talking to another man.

"Yeah, it's the weirdest thing," he said. "Someone got into my truck while I was in the store, emptied all the ashtrays and tidied things up. I have no idea who or why."

She never turned around.

A Husband Unattended

Since my wife retired, she does what many retirees do: whatever she wants.

Like many families, our children and other family members are scattered across the country like dice across a table. Consequently, some of her time is spent flying or driving for visits in Texas, Oklahoma, Virginia and other destinations.

But, being gone from home requires the one thing that most wives dread. Leaving their husbands unattended. For whatever reason, women think that men are completely incapable of handling a few chores in their absence.

So, they leave lists of instructions for you. As if husbands need that much detail for laundry, meals, watering gardens, household cleaning, or taking care of pets.

I resent the assumption that men cannot be trusted to run a household for a handful of days, and that we require a written roadmap to make it through a week or two by ourselves. After all, before I got married, I lived with my mom and dad and got along just fine by myself.

But, I know what will happen if I don't follow the written set of directions she left me. I'll be in trouble. So, following the list is what I'm doing.

According to her laundry notes, I'm supposed to separate the whites into one pile, the darks into another pile, and the towels into another. I did that, but I'm not sure what the point of all that was since I was easily able to cram all of them into one load. However, even though she said to use cold water, I know that hot cleans better, so I turned it to the hot water setting. I also tossed some bleach in there to kill any germs.

Her instructions on heating up these frozen meals just say to, "Follow the directions on the box." I got as far as the temp setting, which is really all you need to know, and put the lasagna in the oven. I probably should have read on down to the part about how long to leave this in the oven, but it's too late now because it's already in there. By the way, these boxes are flammable.

My wife spends a lot of time on her garden, and she is very particular about who she allows to go near it. She babies the plants like children. Her specific instructions were to turn on the soaker hoses for each section for 20 minutes. But, I spotted the two 55-gallon rain barrels and decided to tump them over, flooding all of the garden areas at once. This was done in about one minute, which saved me 19 minutes that I can now spend on more laundry.

Glad I paid attention in math class.

She asked me to dust and vacuum while she was gone. According to these notes, I should use a cloth with the furniture polish and lightly go over each picture frame, shelf, cabinet, and so on, before I vacuum. Realizing this was going to take a ton of time and that I needed to see if the clothes were ready for the dryer, I grabbed the electric leaf blower from the garage and zipped through the house in short order. I was able to blow all of the dust out the back door. Unintentionally, a couple of picture frames and the cat went with it.

Which reminds me, I'm supposed to feed the pets.

The notes say that the goldfish food is to the right of the fish tank, which is where I found it. I'm not sure what this food is made of, but it looks like little flakes of something. It's not very appealing, so I crumbled up a piece of light bread across the top of the water. I remember doing that at the pond when I was a kid, and the fish went nuts. They loved it. I'm sure these guys will too.

146

The cat not only hates the leaf blower, she also doesn't seem to like her mother being gone. She's constantly meowing and weaving around my feet, almost tripping me everywhere I go. The notes say to feed the cat one cup of food a day, but it doesn't say which day. I went ahead and fed her the first day after my wife left. I hope that was the right one.

My wife comes home tomorrow and I'm glad. It's not that I mind having to take care of the house when she's gone, but I don't have the heart to tell her that quite often, men figure out better ways to do things.

There's no way I'll dare tell her that, though. She thinks men are incompetent.

CHAPTER TWELVE – GOD AND COUNTRY

Southern Hospitality

The nicest people live in the South.

Anyone who was born and raised in the South and has done any traveling has probably noticed the same thing that I have: We're friendlier.

Now, I'm not saying that people who live in the north, east or western part of the United States aren't nice folks. I'm simply saying we're friendlier in the South.

I'll give you an example. Only folks in the South can strike up a conversation with a complete stranger in a doctor's office, airport or restaurant, and within minutes be talking about kids or grandkids, church or food.

If food is discussed, it's likely that the women will walk away with at least two recipes scrawled on a napkin or a magazine.

If you try this sort of thing in New York City or Chicago, people look at you as if you want something.

If you've ever ridden mass transportation in a big city, virtually no one talks to anyone else. Subways and buses are fairly quiet, except for the rumbling of the subway tracks or the diesel engine on the bus.

They just don't talk to each other like folks in the South do.

In the South, we say "howdy" to pretty much anyone we see. It's just common courtesy down here. We even greet folks while we're driving.

When I started driving in the mid-'70s in rural Arkansas, I quickly learned that when you passed someone on the road, it was expected that you would lift the fingers on one hand from the steering wheel to acknowledge the other person or persons in the oncoming vehicle.

Most of the men would abbreviate that to raising their index finger. During a recent visit, I noticed that this practice is still in place today.

Also in the South, folks are pretty accepting of family flaws. We all have them. So rather than try to hide them, we openly and nicely discuss lots of things that go on in our own family and in other families. This could include a family member who could easily qualify as the village idiot, or the relative whose front yard looks like a salvage yard for muscle cars.

We don't talk about anyone with malice, and we always end any comments with "Bless their heart," to make it OK.

If we're honest, everyone's family is just a couple of cousins away from being on "The Jerry Springer Show."

Also, if you live in the South, when someone in your family passes away, there'll be a herd of people at your front door in short order. And, they'll all be bringing enough casseroles, meatloaf, fried chicken, vegetables and desserts to feed an army.

Southern people know why it's called comfort food.

Lots of Northerners retire to the South. Many of them have told me that they moved here because of the weather, but that they were pleasantly surprised at how nice everyone is.

It really is a shame that people being nice to each other is a surprise to anyone. As my momma told me when I was a kid, "Being nice doesn't cost you a thing."

And that's the nice thing about mommas: They're always right.

With the Thanks of a Grateful Nation

I sat near the front of the auditorium. I was the fourth to speak, so I wanted to be as near to the podium as possible. But, I sat in the section to the left. The center area was for the veterans.

There were only two.

It was the 74th memorial service for the Camp Fannin Association, and it was held at UT Health Northeast, which now occupies the site of one of the largest military training facilities of the Second World War. I was asked to give part of the welcome.

I did some quick math in my head. If these two gentlemen were, say, 17 or 18 years old when they were at Camp Fannin between 1943 and 1946, they are probably 90 or older today.

I'm a huge fan and student of history, and there was much I learned that day about Camp Fannin and about all of those who were at the camp to train before they were sent to the front lines to defend our country.

For many, it was a one-way trip.

After the Japanese attacked Pearl Harbor in 1941, the men and women of what former news anchor Tom Brokaw appropriately called, "The Greatest Generation," mobilized and geared up in very short order to fight for our freedom and our future.

Factories that made automobiles were quickly converted to build Jeeps, planes and other needed mechanized tools of war.

Women left the home to work the jobs that were vacated by the men who enlisted. Many of those men who enlisted came to Camp Fannin.

Just as the factories were converted for the war effort, the United States government took 14,000 acres near what is now the area on Highways 271 and 155, and in six months, built 600 barracks, a hospital, roads, and all of the other things needed for a training facility for soldiers.

Former Smith County Sheriff J.B. Smith was the featured speaker at the memorial ceremony, and he showed photos and shared many of the stats about Camp Fannin.

As many as 40,000 men at once were at Camp Fannin, he said. Estimates put the total number of men who trained at the U.S. Army Infantry Replacement Training Center at around 200,000.

In 1944, 16,000 soldiers were marched from Camp Fannin to downtown Tyler. The march circled the town square and then made its way back to the camp.

At that time, it was one of the largest military marches in the country.

I thought about what that must've been like to witness. Before television, events such as this would've only been available as a photograph in the newspaper or a radio report. It had to be quite amazing to see.

Many of those who are from the Tyler area who were here during the short time that Camp Fannin was here are now gone. So, all that remains of events such as the march are the photographs.

There were other photos of a wartime Christmas. What appeared to be one of the barracks had the letters, "Merry Christmas" sitting on the roof with lights to illuminate them.

There were many pictures of military generals standing and inspecting troops. They were watching the enlisted men training, firing weapons, and in one photo, pushing a Jeep out of the mud.

As J.B. pointed out, the enlisted men always got the grunt work. I'm sure they still do.

As I listened, I glanced back at the two Camp Fannin veterans. They were quiet and attentive. I tried to imagine what was going through their minds. They were seeing photos from this period in their lives. Did they remember when these were taken? Were they there for any of the events we were seeing?

Americans weren't the only ones here in East Texas at that time. German prisoners of war were also held at the camp.

Just two days before the memorial service, a large model ship, built by a German POW, was donated to the Camp Fannin Association by the daughter of a lieutenant who had served at the camp.

The German built the model from things he had available. The ship is on loan to UT Health and is on display there.

For a few years, East Texas was the destination for thousands. Some who came willingly, and others who were captured and held. But, each person was someone's son, brother or husband.

The Camp Fannin Association works to keep their sacrifice and the memory of what they did alive. We owe it to those who came before us to support their efforts and to learn our own community's history.

I was honored to be a part of the memorial and to learn more about the thousands of heroes who called Tyler home as they trained to put their lives on the line for their fellow man and future generations.

Only a few are still with us. This day there were two.

Goodness

Canton, Texas has a special place in my heart. When I was a kid, my family and I made monthly trips to Canton's First Monday Trade Days.

As I write this, the tornadoes of April 29, 2017, are just hours behind us.

My wife and I were fortunate. Where we live was spared. Our fellow East Texans in Canton and other towns were not.

Canton was hit by four twisters, and Grand Saline by one.

There was loss of life and loss of homes and property.

As I look out of the bay window of our home, the sun is shining and the air is calm and crisp. A stark contrast from what I saw though the same panes a half day previous.

What I'm feeling is a mixture of sadness and empathy.

But, I am also filled with pride. I am witnessing how much good is inside of people.

Before the weather turned ominous, those who work at the National Weather Service, in the news media, and the amateur radio operators, did what they do best. They manned their stations and went to work.

Days prior, those who forecast warned that severe weather was possible. As it formed, ham radio operators joined the emergency weather frequency and reported what they saw and heard. This information was shared with the weather service and the news outlets.

Ham operators aren't paid. During emergencies, while others are taking cover, they stare down ugly weather and other dangerous events so that others can be warned.

The news media did an outstanding job. Television and radio stations reported almost nonstop. Newspapers did the same on the internet and social media.

Social media, such as Facebook and Twitter, has brought the general public into a role that they previously couldn't play: Reporter.

Within minutes of the first twisters, videos, photos, and information was flowing through social media. It allowed families who were caught in the affected areas to let relatives and friends know that they were OK. It also helped those responding to the disasters know where they were needed.

Many of our first responders, like ham operators, are also volunteers. Those who are members of the volunteer fire departments do what they do because they want to. Often, at their own expense. It was the faces of these men and women that we saw responding to help those who needed them.

A good human being is someone goes toward danger instead of away from it.

We watched videos of these responders climbing under overturned cars and trucks, searching houses that were only half there, and wading through mud-filled pastures, looking for someone who was waiting for their assistance.

Those of us who call this part of the United States home know that tornadoes are part of living here.

Just as those on the West Coast endure earthquakes, and coastal residents deal with hurricanes, we know that this type of severe weather goes with the territory.

Many of us have been through and even in a tornado. But we don't let it beat us.

We do what we always do. We help each other. We clean up, and we rebuild.

We are doing it now, and we'll do it again.

I was always taught that most people are inherently good. Sometimes, I doubt that. But, tragic events such as April 29 restore my faith in humanity.

When tragedy strikes, we want answers. Sometimes, there are none.

This is where faith steps in. Because without faith in tragedy, there is little hope.

Picturing Grace

When I was a child, there was a painting that hung on my grandmother's kitchen wall. It portrayed a man who was praying over a meal of bread and what appeared to be a bowl of soup. Near the man was a book, which I always assumed was a Bible, and a pair of spectacles.

From my earliest recollections until my dad's mother passed, I remember looking at this painting while we ate in her home and wondering many things. Who was the man in the painting? Was he a real man or did he originate in the artist's imagination? How old was the painting?

I never asked my grandmother about the image. Honestly, it never occurred to me that one day it would matter much. But something happened recently that changed that.

Several months ago, I expressed on my Facebook page that the painting meant a lot to me. I don't recall if someone had posted a photo of it or how I came to make the comment, but my aunt saw my post and messaged me.

She owns a resale shop in my hometown and said that she could get me a copy of it. I offered to pay her, but she wouldn't let me. She had also shared family meals in the same kitchen and remembered the photo.

After my aunt acquired a framed copy for me and my mom picked it up and delivered it during a recent visit, I did some homework on the painting.
I was surprised by what I learned.

The painting isn't a painting. It is a photograph.

The Bible isn't a Bible. It is a dictionary.

There's more.

Here's how the story goes:

Somewhere between 1918 and 1920, the photo was reportedly taken in a studio in Bovey, Minnesota, by a man named Eric Enstrom. However, the date of the photo is in question because Enstrom's daughter, who was born in 1917, claimed that she remembered it being taken.

Regardless of the date discrepancy, we do know that the man in the photo was named Charles Wilden. According to a number of online sources, Wilden was a Swedish immigrant who lived in Grand Rapids, Minnesota, a city located about 8 miles from Bovey. He made his living as a peddler. According to one account, Wilden stopped by Enstrom's studio to sell shoe-scrapers and was convinced to pose for a photo.

Enstrom placed the dictionary, food, silverware, and the eyeglasses on the table and had Wilden bow his head in prayer. He then took the photo.

Enstrom said that when he developed the picture, he knew he had something special.

An excerpt from the website gracebyenstrom.com:

"There was something about the old gentleman's face that immediately impressed me. I saw that he had a kind face... there weren't any harsh lines in it," Enstrom recalled of Charles Wilden's 1918 visit to his studio.

It happened that Enstrom, at that time, was preparing a portfolio of pictures to take with him to a convention of the Minnesota Photographers Association. "I wanted to take a picture that would show people that, even though they had to do without many things because of the war, they still had much to be thankful for," he said.

According the site, Enstrom said he felt the photo seemed to be saying, "This man doesn't have much of earthly goods, but he has more than most people because he has a thankful heart."

The U.S. had just reluctantly entered World War I and, understandably, everyone was worried and fearful.

At first, Enstrom made one print at a time and put them in the window of his photo studio. The copies sold quickly. He made more. Many more.

Enstrom's daughter would later hand-color copies of the photo, which is the version that most of us recognize today. Soon, that version would be seen, loved and sold throughout the world.

In 1926, Enstrom paid Wilden for all rights to the photo. One online entry mentions that after that contractual agreement, Wilden was not seen again. No one knows his fate.

A modest salesman from a small Minnesota town likely lived the remainder of his days feeling that his life had been of minimal importance. Yet, nothing could be further from the truth.

Charles Wilden attained an immorality that few ever do. But, it isn't his name that is immortal. It is his brief action in front of a camera almost 100 years ago that God used to send a message of faith for generations to come.

A message of faith that resonated with millions, including my grandmother. A message of her faith, and later mine, that was conveyed to me through a powerful photo that hung on her kitchen wall.

A photo that I now own. A photo simply titled, "Grace."

About John Moore

John Moore is a former radio personality and the owner of One Moore Production, a multi-media company. You can reach him through his website at johnmoore.net.

Made in the USA
Coppell, TX
29 November 2020